Praise for *Flagging the Problem*

In Flagging the Pr[...] *unique approach to* [...] *coded flag system: t[...] mood system, the Red Flag stands for depression, the Yellow Flag for anxiety, the Purple Flag for addiction, and the White Flag for suicide.*

Above all, he seeks to dispel the stigma that continues to surround mental illness.

"This is an important book. It provides a new approach to mental health and the intricacy of the variables that influence it. Written with compassion and creativity and informed by decades of General Practice insights, Dr Harry Barry helps the reader to understand the complexity of the normal mood system and the distress of depression, anxiety, addiction and suicide.'

Marie Murray, Director of the Student Counselling Services at University College Dublin

'It's that rare thing – a medical book that can be read by lay people and health professionals alike. Dr Barry demystifies subjects that touch so many of our lives and he does so with compassion, wisdom and vast professional knowledge.' WITHDRAWN

Cathy Kelly

Praise for *Flagging the Therapy*

Flagging the Therapy *focuses on two of the most common mental-health problems: depression and anxiety. Dr Barry examines the range of options, including the various drug, talk and alternative therapies, available to those suffering from depression and anxiety, whether mild or severe. Drawing on his extensive experience as a GP of 'walking the walk' with those on such a journey, he outlines a new holistic pathway which is practical and easy to follow.*

'Dr Barry's first book was truly unique. In *Flagging the Therapy*, he develops his highly acces[...] KILKENNY COUNTY LIBRARY [...]ith a particular emphasis on how diffe[...] [...]xiety and other

psychological problems work. Another superb contribution from one of Ireland's most insightful doctors.'
Dr Muiris Houston, Medical Correspondent, the *Irish Times*

'Once again, Dr Barry has achieved his goal of removing the barriers that deter people from seeking professional help due to embarrassment or lack of knowledge. He is to be lauded for this.'
Prof. Patricia Casey, Department of Psychiatry, University College Dublin

'Dr Barry has done medicine and mental health a great service by writing an authoritative yet accessible exposition on cutting-edge thinking relating to recovery from states of anxiety and depression. This is a remarkable achievement but, more importantly, the book is a reliable field guide for patients and practitioners alike. The Salmon of Knowledge has revisited the Boyne! I strongly recommend that you read this book.'
Dr Justin Brophy, President, The College of Psychiatry of Ireland

'This is a truly ground-breaking, innovative and profoundly enlightening work. Dr Harry Barry leads the reader on a holistic journey through the mind and its emotional responses in a way that is both explorative and explanatory. Brilliantly written, it is essential reading for anyone who wants to develop a comprehensive knowledge of effective approaches to positive mental health in our society.'
Maria Carmody, President, National Counselling Institute of Ireland (NCII)

'In this intelligent and enlightening study, Dr Barry has managed to combine everyday stories with an easily understood discussion on the neurobiological basis of mental ill-health. His nonjudgemental attitude to the various therapies which are at our disposal for recovery and his holistic approach to mental and spiritual well-being are revolutionary. *Flagging the Therapy* is not just a book for sufferers of mental illness; it is mandatory reading for all those who have the slightest interest in good health and human happiness.'
Carol Hunt, *Sunday Independent*

FLAGGING STRESS

First published in 2010 by
Liberties Press
Guinness Enterprise Centre | Taylor's Lane | Dublin 8
Tel: +353 (1) 415 1224
www.LibertiesPress.com | info@libertiespress.com

Distributed in the United States by
Dufour Editions | PO Box 7 | Chester Springs
Pennsylvania | 19425 | USA

and in Australia by
James Bennett Pty Limited | InBooks | 3 Narabang Way
Belrose NSW 2085 | Australia

Trade enquiries to Gill & Macmillan Distribution
Hume Avenue | Park West | Dublin 12
Tel: +353 (1) 500 9534 | Fax: +353 (1) 500 9595
www.gillmacmillan.ie

ISBN: 978-1-905483-31-0
2 4 6 8 10 9 7 5 3 1
A CIP record for this title is available from the British Library.

Cover design by Sin É Design
Internal design by Liberties Press
Printed in Ireland by Colour Books

FLAGGING STRESS

Toxic Stress and How to Avoid It

Dr Harry Barry

This book is dedicated to my mother, Dilly Barry (1922–2010)

'The butterfly has flown!'

Contents

Acknowledgements

There are so many people that have played a part in making this book possible. As always, I would like to start by thanking my editor Seán O'Keeffe (and his background staff) of Liberties Press for suggesting the book, seeing its potential and creating order out of my ramblings. I also thank Peter O'Connell of Liberties for his wise advice at crucial stages of writing the text and his help with media and marketing.

I must particularly mention my friend and colleague Enda Murphy and his invaluable assistance. Apart from being an intrepid adventurer (having driven all the way from Ireland to China!), he is a wonderful therapist and teacher. I have to thank his lovely wife Mei for putting up with the pair of us.

To my loyal and devoted staff at 5 Leland Place – Fiona, Carmel, Susan, Anne and my practice nurse Brenda – for all their help and support throughout the period of writing this book. I am indeed fortunate to have such a wonderful team at my back. To my mother Dilly Barry (Thurles), who has just lost her long battle with illness (which she had faced with bravery and courage), and my brothers Gerald and Kevin and in-laws Patricia, Una and Nora for their support and encouragement. To my mother-in-law Ciss Lahart (Eyrecourt), who also has shown great courage in coping with illness, for her help and support down through the years, and to all our friends and relatives who have backed this project.

There are a number of people who sadly will not be here to see this published. The first is my brother David. We still miss you. The second is our great family friend Sister Kieran Saunders MMM, who is mentioned in my last book. We miss you so much Kieran, and pray that you will remain our 'spiritual guide' throughout this mysterious journey through the pathways of life and beyond. We also remember my father Harry and father-in-law Nicholas, who are sadly not with us to share this moment.

I have to give special credit to my son Daniel, who, as always, has been my right-hand man throughout the writing and editing of this book. His research background in psychology has been invaluable, and his superb diagrams adorn and enhance this book. Without his help, it would have been impossible to put it all together. I am indeed very proud of him, as I am of my son Joseph, who begins an exciting post doc research post in Germany, and my newlywed daughter Lara, whose love and caring nourishes us all. A special welcome to her new husband Hans, the light of her life! Luscious vegetables from his plot continue to find their way to our table!

I reserve as always my biggest 'thank you' to my wife Brenda, whose love, friendship, support, encouragement and particularly patience have made this book possible. Writing is a lonely experience not only for the author but also for loved ones, who have to endure the author's 'absences' when writing. A book on stress has indeed been a 'stressful' influence on this mad household. Your love has sustained me through it all.

Life is a mysterious journey full of twists and unexpected turns. If you are fortunate enough to have a special companion travelling with you on the way, it becomes an even richer experience. Sometimes there is pain and difficulty; sometimes there is joy. Who knows where the journey is going to bring us, but with you by my side, I know all will be well. May God grant us the gift of getting older and wiser together! '*Mo ghra, mo chroi.*'

A Note to Readers

In my two previous books, I dealt in detail with the neurobiology of the brain and its links with mental-health issues like anxiety, depression, addiction and suicide. In both, I included in-depth research data and references. In this book, I have tried to focus mainly on stress itself, and how to deal with it. As a result, I have not included a detailed reading list and have tried to keep the neurobiological data to a minimum. Those who would like to learn more about the neuroscience behind the mental-health issues raised should go back to my previous two books, *Flagging the Problem* and *Flagging the Therapy*.

Flagging Stress is a handbook that will hopefully assist many in understanding and teasing out the main stress issues in their lives. Many will be able to apply the approaches discussed to their own situations and will need no further assistance. Some, however, may want to seek out a counsellor, CBT therapist or family doctor to travel with them on the journey back to mental health. I exhort you to do so if you feel that this will be of assistance. The old adage, 'a problem shared is a problem halved', still resonates!

Some of those who read this book may find themselves in a dark place. Some may feel hopeless or helpless, unable to see any future. Some may even be planning to end the pain and despair they feel. They may feel that they would be doing those close to them a 'favour' by ending their life or they may be too distressed even to consider the consequences for those left behind.

If you are in this state of mind, I exhort you to come forward and look for help. Men in particular find it very difficult to open up and talk about how they feel. The first step, of opening up to somebody you trust, is often extremely hard to do, but it is a crucial one for the journey back to mental health. If you are unable to do this, at the back of this book is a list of excellent groups with telephone numbers and website addresses. *Make that call.* Apart from changing your life, talking to someone may save those close to you from a lifetime of pain and suffering.

All the case histories and individual references in this book are allegorical in nature.

Introduction

The word 'stress' is one of the most commonly used and least-understood buzzwords of modern life. Stress is at least as prevalent now as it was during the boom years of the Celtic Tiger, despite the fact that circumstances for most people have been completely altered since then. Through researching conditions affecting mental health in my previous two books, I have become increasingly convinced that unhealthy forms of stress are perhaps the greatest single threat to our physical and mental well-being. The purpose of this book is to explore this phenomenon in more detail.

I use the term 'toxic', as it adequately describes the harmful effects that stress can lead to. Stress can lead to a host of serious conditions, both physical and psychological. Such physical ailments include heart attacks, cancer, diabetes, strokes and infertility, while psychological effects of stress include depression and suicide.

There has recently been a stream of high-profile cases in the media, sport and business which have revealed the tragic consequences of toxic stress in the lives of well-known public figures. However, chronic stress can affect people from all walks of life, and has become endemic in modern Ireland. Because many of us are unaware of the presence of chronic stress in our lives, or of just how damaging it can be, we fail to confront this silent menace.

The first part of this book aims to define what stress is, and how it can take on unhealthy aspects. I will explain the evolutionary origins of stress, the impact it has on our bodies and brain, and the fact that our behavioural response to it can be as damaging as the stress itself. I will also explain why some of us are more vulnerable to stress and its effects than others, and will argue that it is crucially important to teach children skills to help them cope with stress from an early age.

In the second part of the book, I will present a seven-step programme which is designed to help identify unhealthy stress in our lives. This programme includes methods that can be used to 'detoxify' stress, in particular changes in thinking and behaviour. I will put forward numerous case studies involving highly stressful situations in everyday life, and show how the people involved learned to reduce their levels of harmful stress to a healthier level.

Readers may notice a strong emphasis in this book on the links between stress and suicide; I make no excuses for placing this issue squarely in the centre of the discussion. We are in the middle of a crisis in Ireland, not only in economic terms but also in terms of the loss of hundreds of young and not so young lives due to suicide. The greater the stress being put on our young men in particular, the more likely it is that depression, self-harm and death by suicide will emerge, resulting in lifetimes of sadness and guilt for those left behind.

Learning to identify and cope with toxic stress can lead to a happier and more contented life, reduce the risks of a host of physical illnesses like heart attacks, strokes and cancer, and, in some cases, save lives by lessening the curse of young male suicide in Ireland.

Part One

Experts in the field of stress define the phenomenon in a different way to the layperson. To the latter, anything they find difficult in their lives is described as stressful, but stress itself is poorly understood. Even within the fields of science and medicine, there exist numerous definitions of stress, depending on the perspective being taken. It is unsurprising, therefore, that the term is so often misused.

The key difficulty is that we usually don't separate the cause of our stress (the *stressor*) from the activation of our body's stress system (the *stress response*). Stress refers to the latter, so it can be defined as 'the reaction of our stress system to an internal or external stressor'. This is an important distinction, as it implies that stress can be healthy or unhealthy, depending on how the stress system responds to a particular situation.

In practice, most people use the term 'stress' in a purely negative sense, to describe situations where a particular stressor renders them unable to cope, leading to a host of negative physical and mental symptoms. This experience is referred to as 'being stressed'.

A simple example would be Jim, who is going to attend a job interview in a week's time. He feels edgy, his muscles are tense, and his stomach is in knots. While Jim finds these sensations uncomfortable, they are not unhealthy. In this case, the stress response is a natural reaction to the upcoming interview, and its purpose is to help Jim perform to an optimal level.

This type of stress is short-term, or 'acute', and is generally not harmful. Stress can be acute or chronic, healthy or unhealthy, depending on both the length of time for which we experience it and its effects on our physical and mental well-being. Usually, toxic stress occurs when our stress response is chronic and unhealthy. Our mental interpretation of a stressor is just as important as the stressor itself. In the example above, Jim's interpretation that he will not be sufficiently prepared for his interview is leading him into as much trouble as the interview itself.

Our Stress System

Throughout human evolution, survival has been the highest priority. As threats to that survival were mainly physical ones, we developed fast responses and reactions to deal with dangers in our environment. The whole body had to be able to gear up instantly to face such threats, and our internal stress system developed to cope with these demands. Our stress system needed to remain on high alert until such threats had passed. This system would switch off when it was not needed, during periods of inactivity or relaxation.

Three different situations could trigger the stress response in our ancestors. First, one needed to fight to defend against a threat to oneself or one's family. Secondly, where fighting would be unlikely to be successful, one would flee to ensure survival. In the third case, where life was in danger for a longer period of time, through food scarcity or sustained attack from enemies, the stress system would need to remain constantly active. In each scenario, the stress system would help facilitate the appropriate response until one was no longer in danger and survival was assured. This response was controlled by the brain, which chose to switch the stress response on or off depending on what was happening in the environment

Even though most of us no longer encounter such life-threatening situations in our daily lives, the structure, function and organisation of the stress system has changed little from the early period of human evolution. What *has* changed, however, is the nature of the stressors that exist today. While we don't face such acute and obvious dangers as our ancestors did, the challenges presented to us today are less clear-cut, making it difficult for the body to react with an appropriate stress response, resulting in a prolonged activation of our stress system. The stress response was only ever intended as a short-term emergency state of increased alertness, whereas the stress people experience today is long-lasting. Our bodies did not evolve to cope with such chronic stress, and it poses serious risks to our health. In short, the stress system that ensured the survival of our ancestors is threatening our lives today.

Another important difference between the stress experienced by our ancestors and stress as we know it today is the way in which we cope with it. In ancient times, human beings were generally fit and active, and this helped 'burn off' symptoms of stress. In modern times, however, many of us do not exercise, and our response to stress is often to over-eat, drink alcohol and smoke cigarettes – all of which are detrimental to our physical and mental well-being.

To understand why unnecessary and prolonged activation of the stress system can lead to long-term unhealthy effects, we first need to examine the stress system itself.

The Brain's Response to Stress

The prefrontal cortex, or the 'logical brain', is located at the front of our brain; in the middle of our brain sits the limbic system, or 'emotional brain' (see Figure 1). Our behaviour is heavily influenced by the flow of information between these two areas. The part of the brain which controls our stress system is called the amygdala, or 'stress box', and is part of the emotional brain (see Figure 2). When under attack from an internal or external stressor, the stress box is able to activate the body's physical response. Our ultimate response to a stressor, however, will be determined by the interaction between our logical and emotional brain. If the stress system is activated, the stress box releases small messengers within the brain that result in both nervous-system and hormonal responses. I will now look at these responses in more detail, and give three everyday examples to demonstrate how they work.

The Nervous System Response

This response involves the activation of a system of nerves which reach almost every organ in the body, called the *autonomic nervous system* (ANS). This system is essential for our survival, as organs such as the heart, lungs and gut are being constantly monitored and activated by it. The system consists of two components, both of which play a major role in the stress response. The first of these is the *sympathetic nervous system* (SNS); its function is to 'hype up' the body in order to cope with stressors. Its activation is responsible for our acute symptoms of stress: it prompts a faster heartbeat, dry mouth, an unsettled feeling in the gut, dilated pupils and sweating. The system prepares our body to 'fight or flee' in response to a threat by temporarily diverting energy away from non-essential functions such as digestion, and towards the muscles, heart and lungs.

The second system is called the *parasympathetic nervous system* (PNS); its function is to calm us down when we are not under stress. It slows the heartbeat to a normal pace, allows digestion of food, and relaxes our muscles: the 'rest and digest' functions.

The response of the SNS to stress is straightforward: the nerves directly activate all organs which may be able to assist in dealing with the stressor. This system also leads to the activation of a secondary hormonal response.

The Hormonal Response

This is activated by the brain when the stress box sends messengers to the hypothalamus/pituitary gland, or 'hormone control box' (see Figure 3). This in turn sends hormones into the bloodstream and on to the adrenal glands, which sit on top of the kidneys (see Figure 4). The adrenal glands are at the heart of our stress response. Each adrenal gland consists of a central core called the adrenal medulla and an outer shell called the adrenal cortex. The adrenal medulla produces our two acute stress hormones, adrenalin and noradrenalin, and is activated by the SNS. The adrenal cortex, by contrast, is strongly activated by hormones sent from the brain and produces the chronic stress hormone glucocortisol.

These stress hormones are then released into the bloodstream and travel around the body to further activate organs involved in the stress response, such as the heart, lungs and gut. Each of the stress hormones plays a different role in the stress response.

ADRENALIN is released when we encounter an acutely stressful situation where we feel fear and our natural response is to flee. An example would be where we are confronted with someone wielding a knife and demanding our wallet! Adrenalin is also the hormone released during a panic attack.

NORADRENALIN is released when we encounter an acutely stressful situation where our feeling is anger and our response is aggression. An example would be where we may try to wrestle the knife from our attempted mugger! How we handle acute stress – whether we fight or flee – depends on the relative amount of adrenalin or noradrenalin released into our system.

GLUCOCORTISOL is released when we encounter a stressful situation that persists for a long period of time. Its function is to provide the energy required to keep the stress response active as long as it is needed. As we will see later, the production of consistently high levels of this hormone over an extended period of time results in many of the serious consequences of toxic stress.

To summarise, when we encounter acute stress, the brain decides on the appropriate response through interaction between its logical and emotional areas. The stress box is activated, and this switches on the SNS. If the response is to flee, the SNS instructs the adrenal gland to produce adrenalin, and we prepare to run, with fear being the emotion experienced. If the response is to fight, the adrenal gland releases noradrenalin, with the emotion experienced being anger. If the stress becomes chronic, the stress box sends information through the hormone control box, instructing the adrenal gland to produce glucocortisol to prolong the stress response. The role of our PNS is to allow the stress system to take a breather and encourage the body to relax. Without the PNS, we would live in such a state of acute stress that we would quickly burn out.

Here are three examples of our stress system in action.

EXAMPLE 1

Mary is returning home late at night. She is close to home when she notices a man hanging around across the road. He has a hood up over his head and appears to be watching her intently. Her logical and emotional brains go into overdrive. She feels afraid, and experiences an instinctive desire to run the last few yards to her front door. Her SNS is activated, which encourages the adrenal gland to pour out adrenalin into her bloodstream. Her heart rate soars, her breathing becomes shallower, her pupils dilate, she begins to sweat, and her stomach clenches tightly. All of these things prepare her for a bolt to her front door – which she succeeds in doing. On entering her house, she meets her brother and begins to relax, until eventually her adrenalin levels return to normal. In this situation, her natural stress reaction has potentially saved her from danger.

EXAMPLE 2

Dave is coming home with his girlfriend when he encounters an aggressive youth who threatens them both. As he feels he must protect his girlfriend, his stress system is activated in a different manner to Mary's in the previous example. His logical and emotional brains decide on an action other than fleeing. He experiences anger, and his stress box activates the SNS, which in turn releases noradrenalin into the bloodstream. His senses are heightened, his face displays aggression, his heart rate rises, his muscles tense, and he is poised to strike his assailant. He fends off the threat until his attacker flees. His acute stress response in this situation allows him to neutralise a threat to himself and his girlfriend.

EXAMPLE 3

Peter is called in to see his boss, who explains that the financial situation in the company is very challenging and that he cannot guarantee that Peter's job will be there by the new year, which is only four months away. When Peter hears the news, his stress system starts to pour out adrenalin due to the shock, and he feels fearful. As time goes by, his stress system begins to produce large amounts of glucocortisol. He starts to suffer from fatigue, broken sleep and poor concentration. He loses interest and enjoyment in life and feels constantly on edge, tense and worried. He describes the way he feels to his wife as 'tired but wired'. He suffers from cold sores and chest infections. He turns to alcohol to cope, but this only makes matters worse. He starts to feel down. All of these symptoms are indicators of chronic stress and are attributable to the persistently high levels of glucocortisol present in his system. Fortunately, when the new year arrives, his boss calls him in to tell him that his job is secure. After a few days, his stress system calms down, his glucocortisol levels finally wane, and his physical and mental health begin to recover.

In the first two examples, acute stress enabled the individuals to deal with threats. However, as can be seen in the third example, when the stress response becomes excessive and prolonged, we become unable to cope with the physical and mental demands that are placed on us. This is when stress becomes unhealthy, or toxic. The next section will examine the biological and behavioural consequences that result from this type of stress.

Let's start by examining the possible negative effects of the individual stress hormones.

Noradrenalin

Of the two acute stress hormones, this is the one which is of most concern. It is released when our reaction to stress is either anger or frustration. Some people always respond to stress in this way. This hormone poses a number of potentially dangerous consequences to our vascular system, including:

- heart attacks in those with known or unidentified coronary heart disease

- serious electrical disturbances within the heart (arrhythmias), which can lead to sudden death
- a rise in blood cholesterol, increasing the risk of angina and heart attacks
- a rise in blood pressure, which is a risk factor in stroke and angina, and
- alterations in blood circulation in arteries leading to the brain, also increasing the risk of stroke.

Individuals who continuously respond to stress with anger and frustration are therefore more likely to put their health at risk. For this at-risk group, reducing the risk of vascular incidents will involve retraining their response to stress.

Adrenalin

This hormone is released when our stress response is fear or anxiety. Although the symptoms associated with an excessive release of adrenalin are extremely unpleasant, they are not as dangerous as those associated with noradrenalin.

Glucocortisol

This hormone is released in large amounts in chronic stress, and is responsible for the mental and physical symptoms which appear when stress becomes toxic. A large volume of research has built up to show that this is harmful to both our body and mind in the following ways:

- increased blood sugar and diabetes
- increased cholesterol and triglycerides (blood fats), which increase the risk of heart attack and stroke

- higher levels of blood platelets, increasing the risk of heart attack and stroke
- damage to white blood cells, leading to viral and bacterial infections and reducing the body's ability to detect and destroy cancer cells, which are constantly being produced within the body
- shedding of calcium in bones, resulting in a risk of developing osteoporosis (thinning of the bones)
- increased sensitivity to pain due to a depletion of endorphins in the brain
- unhealthy weight loss or gain, depending on how the stress response affects appetite
- insomnia and resulting fatigue, and
- decreased libido and decreased fertility in men and women.

The effects of high levels of glucocortisol on the immune system are worth examining in more detail. The natural pattern is higher levels of glucocortisol during the daytime and lower levels at night, but this is disrupted at times of chronic stress. During the day, our immune system tends to neutralise viruses and bacteria, and at night it helps destroy cancer cells. Consistently high levels of glucocortisol for a prolonged period of time disrupt these functions, making us prone to infections and less efficient in destroying cancer cells.

The main psychological consequences of chronically high levels of glucocortisol are as follows:

- mental fatigue (often misdiagnosed as physical fatigue)
- anxiety is common in the beginning of chronic stress, eventually leading to apathy

- damage to the mood system, which can trigger bouts of depression. High levels of glucocortisol during a person's childhood may damage key brain pathways, predisposing them to depression in later life (For more on this, see *Flagging the Therapy*.)
- increased risk of suicide
- reduced capacity for enjoying life, and
- unhealthy behavioural responses, which exacerbate the problem.

Most of the harmful effects of acute stress can be attributed to noradrenalin, and these effects are usually experienced by individuals who respond to stress with anger. However, it is important to note that this group can also succumb to the effects of glucocortisol if the stress becomes prolonged. It is clear from the above list that stress can be highly damaging to both body and mind, and potentially fatal.

Our behaviour in response to stress is of the utmost importance and will ultimately influence how stress affects our health. Unfortunately, often our natural response to persistent stress is to involve ourselves in a range of negative behaviours. Here are some of the more common and destructive ones:

- Smokers increasing the amount of cigarettes smoked per day, which further increases the risk of heart attack, stroke and lung cancer;
- Serious misuse and abuse of alcohol to numb the physical and psychological symptoms of stress. This increases the risk of depression, suicide, addiction, liver disease and mouth cancer;
- Avoiding exercise due to physical and mental fatigue, leading to obesity;

- Changes in eating habits, with a risk of developing anorexia or obesity. When obesity is combined with high levels of glucocortisol, diabetes can follow. Eating highly processed foods because we don't have the energy to cook properly increases our risk of bowel cancer;

- Drinking caffeine, Coke or energy drinks to try and relieve fatigue, which increases the risks of anxiety, obesity and diabetes;

- Some will respond with aggressive behaviour, such as road rage or fighting following an alcohol binge. This may lead to serious injury and impulsive violent acts towards themselves or others;

- Some may turn to illegal drugs such as cocaine or hash to cope with persistent stress, despite the obvious dangers associated with these substances. Others may begin to misuse prescription drugs, such as tranquillizers, and become addicted to them.

As we can see, when the stress response is inappropriate, it can lead to a range of behaviours which threaten our physical and psychological well-being.

The brain is highly plastic and adaptable; prolonged exposure to persistent toxic levels of stress leads the brain to amplify our stress response so that we begin to live in a constant state of hyper-vigilance. This results in an over-production of noradrenalin and glucocortisol in particular – and all the risks that this entails. To reverse this process, we must encourage the brain to 'turn down the volume'!

Toxic stress can also be triggered by boredom or inactivity. In my line of work, I see many men suffering heart attacks or cancers shortly after retiring. I feel that it is their inability to adapt to their new lifestyle that is triggering such illnesses. It is possible that high levels of glucocortisol underlie these health problems.

The brain is the boss of our stress system and is responsible for analysing the stressors in our lives. If we expose the brain to persistently high levels of unhealthy stress, it will 'reset the system' and result in chronic stress.

However, the brain can be encouraged to revert back to normal. It is the plastic, or changeable, nature of the brain which helps us deal with toxic stress.

The Anatomy of Toxic Stress

Now that we have an understanding of our stress response, and in particular how 'toxic stress' can be so damaging to our physical and mental health, let's turn our attention to the mechanisms which underlie the stress response. For stress to become harmful, four conditions are necessary:

- The stressor involved must be significant to us;
- This stressor must be either chronic (present for a significant period of time) or involve regular periods of significant acute severe stress to become a problem. This usually happens because we are unable to deal with the stressor;
- It must overpower our innate resilience to stress, triggering the cascade of physical and psychological consequences already discussed;
- It must be accompanied by unhealthy behaviour patterns that worsen the problem.

Let's take another example. John has worked in a company for many years and is quite happy with his job. A new manager is appointed; he wants to completely revamp the workplace.

John struggles with the changes and starts to interpret the situation incorrectly, believing that the manager does not like him and is trying to make his situation untenable in order to be able to let him go. Although this is not the case, it is John's perception of the situation.

Over time, John develops all the symptoms of chronic stress. He becomes increasingly exhausted, anxious, less efficient at work and snappy at home. He loses his usual sense of enjoyment of life and finally becomes apathetic. He starts to drink more at night and stops enjoying food and sex. In particular, he stops doing the one activity that might have helped him deal with his stress: taking exercise. Before his problems began, he had always taken a daily walk, but this fell by the wayside. He finally comes down with a bad viral illness as his immune system becomes compromised. He ends up spending a full month out of work on sick leave. It takes the combined efforts of his GP and a work-based counsellor to get him back on track.

How we view stressors depends on the 'lens' through which we have learned to view life. In the example above, the stressor involved was John's incorrect assumptions about the motives behind his manager's actions. Because he held these assumptions for some time, the stress response began to overpower John's natural resilience, and he moved into the world of toxic stress. We also see how his unhealthy behaviours of drinking, not exercising and eating poorly, together with the chronic stress response itself, led to him developing a viral illness and spending a month out of work.

Let's examine the four conditions necessary for toxic stress in more detail.

1. The stressor (or our interpretation of it) must be of a significant nature

All of us can easily identify many of the major stressors that can occur in our lives. We live in a fast-moving, technologically driven culture where the speed of change over the past decade has been staggering. Our society has been torn apart by the breakdown of traditional and community structures for a variety of social, economic, religious and political reasons. This has resulted in major stressors, some of the most common of which are listed below:

Relationship difficulties are a major source of acute and chronic stress. While separations and divorces are obvious stressors, even simple disagreements between couples can cause tremendous stress for those involved. Family conflicts can also be very stressful, and in many cases may last for years.

Exam pressures are another potent cause of chronic stress – ranging from the state exams, like the Junior and Leaving Certificates, to postgraduate exams. This is largely attributable to the expectations heaped upon students by well-meaning parents, as well as the expectations of the student themselves. This stressor can potentially increase the risks of self-harm.

Loss – particularly the death of someone close to us – is a very powerful stressor and in some cases can have serious physical and psychological consequences. Grief can also result from the loss of a pet or the ending of a relationship.

Work pressures are another major stressor. Bullying in the workplace is one of the most insidious and potentially toxic causes of significant stress. Nowadays, the fear of losing one's job is causing untold damage to the stress systems of many people. For some people, work produces typical adrenalin 'fear responses', and for others noradrenalin 'anger/frustration responses'.

A period of unemployment is a highly stressful time for many people – particularly if, as is often the case in Ireland at the moment, the person is experiencing it for the first time. Unemployment can lead to a significant loss in self-esteem and can generate huge financial pressure, which many people are simply unable to cope with.

Financial difficulties are another significant source of acute and chronic bouts of stress. Debt and difficulties with banks, finance companies and moneylenders are particularly stressful when one is in a precarious financial position. If these difficulties persist, they can threaten the person's physical and mental well-being. We only have to look at our suicide rates to see the dangerous consequences of this stressor.

Housing issues are another common stressor. These stressors, from challenges relating to building or extending a home to struggling to make mortgage repayments and dealing with negative equity and repossession, are likely to remain for decades.

Addiction is another stressor for both the addict and their family. Addiction is so destructive to a person's physical, psychological and social makeup that the stress response produced can be highly toxic.

Illness is highly stressful both for the sufferer and those close to them. Any significant illness challenges our internal stress system. Many result in physical and psychological symptoms and can present huge challenges for family members, as those who look after dementia patients can testify. Some will succumb to toxic stress as a response.

Those who live with significant physical or mental handicap will be prone to stress, and those who look after them can also suffer from stress.

These are obvious significant stressors, but our interpretation of events can also result in toxic stress. Even though a stressor may seem relatively innocuous to others and actually present no real threat to us, it can still result in toxic stress. This may be the single most important factor when it comes to stress. Of all the disciplines, arguably CBT (cognitive behaviour therapy) has been most effective when it comes to dealing with this aspect of stress.

We now know that due to a combination of genetic and early environmental influences, each of us begins to develop internal belief systems through which we evaluate everything that happens to us from day to day. This plays a major role in deciding whether our primary emotional response to acute stress is fear, anger or frustration. This in turn can result in unhealthy behavioural responses.

I covered the 'ABC' system (practiced by CBT therapists and created by the psychotherapist Albert Ellis) in *Flagging the Therapy* and will be dealing with it in more detail later. But here is a summary of this system:

A (ACTIVATING EVENT) Represents the stressor plus our interpretation of why it is bothering us.

B (BELIEFS) Represents our internal belief system/demands

C (CONSEQUENCES) Represents the emotional, physical and behavioural consequences which occur in response to a particular stressor.

To expand on this concept, we can say that our interpretation of the initial stressor is influenced by the underlying belief system we have developed (which usually involves making unrealistic demands on ourselves).

So if I begin to feel extremely stressed about any particular situation or event, analysing it using the 'ABC' system can often quickly reveal how I am feeling and why I am behaving as I am in response to it.

Let's take an example. Peter is becoming stressed. He feels he was passed over for promotion because he was not invited to apply for the post. In fact, his boss has been planning to transfer him to a different department as a promotion but does not want to reveal his hand yet. An 'ABC' analysis of the issue would go like this:

A. Peter does not get invited to apply for the position. He interprets this as a sign that he is not in favour with his boss and may be viewed as having few prospects with the company.

B. Peter looks for certainty that he will not be let go by the company.

C. Peter becomes highly stressed. He initially demonstrates an adrenalin fear/anxiety response but later becomes exhausted and stops sleeping, increases his alcohol intake and spends more and more time worrying about being let go.

In practice, it is Peter's erroneous interpretation of events, and his unrealistic demand that he must not be let go by his company, that is driving his toxic stress response. Crucially, it is often our incorrect analysis of events that triggers such responses. This will form an important component of how we deal with stress, as we will see.

2. The stressor must be either chronic (present for a significant period of time) or involve regular periods of severe, acute stress.

As a general rule, stress only becomes toxic when we are exposed to persistent bouts of acute or chronic stress. An example of acute stress might be where we are intermittently exposed to episodes of bullying at work, and chronic stress might be where we lose our job and struggle to make ends meet over the subsequent year. Our stress system is usually quite robust and able to deal with less intense episodes of stress; exposure to significant or constant stressors puts us most at risk.

The stress system is engaged to deal with, and hopefully eliminate, the stressor. But as we all know, there are many situations in life where this is simply not possible, and so our stress system is forced to stay on high alert – with potentially dangerous results. Sometimes it is our own unhealthy belief system that may be driving the stress response: unless we get help to deal with this, the stress system will remain in overdrive.

A simple way of looking at the above is to regard our stress response as being controlled by a 'stress thermostat'. If we are exposed to long periods of persistent stress, the thermostat dial is set at a higher level – leading to toxic stress, and its consequences. Resetting the thermostat downwards will be one of the main planks of any successful approach to tackling the problem.

3. The stressor must overpower our innate resilience to stress

One of the most important concepts of mental health is that we are all different in the way we perceive and handle stress. We have known for decades that our genes and upbringing combine to create our individual innate resilience to stress. In practice, this means that some of us cope better, both physically and mentally, with the 'slings and arrows' life throws at us. Genes like the 'Resilience Gene', which I discussed in *Flagging the Therapy*, play a key role in our potential vulnerability to stress. However, the environmental conditions pertaining to our development as babies, children, teenagers and young adults also play an important role in determining whether such genes are expressed.

Irrespective of our capacity to cope with stress, most of us, during certain periods of our lives, will feel that our world is 'falling in', and will end up battling the host of negative and unhealthy consequences which follow. For some of us, it may take major stressors to trigger such difficulties, but for others who are more vulnerable, relatively minor incidents may overwhelm our natural defences.

It must be emphasised that normal levels of stress are healthy and well tolerated by the brain and body. It is only when our response to a stressor is major and prolonged that our resilience may be overwhelmed.

4. The stressor must be accompanied by unhealthy behaviours

For stress to be harmful, or toxic, associated unhealthy behavioural patterns are generally involved. This is because we struggle to deal with the negative mental and physical consequences of a stress response which has become prolonged, chronic and harmful to the body. In order to cope, we often turn to unhealthy behaviours such as smoking and alcohol misuse, and cease healthy behaviours such as eating properly and exercising.

Stress: The Modern View

Understanding the modern approach to stress requires knowledge of concepts such as:

- contentment
- social support systems
- optimal stress levels
- lack of goals, and
- the importance of dignity.

CONTENTMENT relates to the acceptance of oneself and one's life circumstances. There are likely to be situations where we lose our sense of contentment. This is often due to unrealistic expectations. Our expectations are often based on what we have learned when growing and developing as people, and may encourage us to build up mental pictures of where we 'should be', which are often different from where we actually are. Although we may feel that these aspirations are reasonable and achievable, they are often unrealistic and counterproductive. Sometimes we expect too much of ourselves, and demand too much from our situation. The more we demand such changes, the more stress we are likely to feel. By contrast, if we take a more pragmatic approach and accept that the world is unlikely to change to suit us any time soon, we are far less likely to experience the toxic effects of stress, and more likely to feel content with ourselves and our lives.

There is little doubt that the recent prolonged period of economic prosperity in Ireland threatened our sense of contentment due to its overemphasis on material possessions. The economic situation today challenges contentment for a markedly different reason: many of us are now struggling to make ends meet, or are adjusting to the fact of having a lower standard of living. How we cope in either scenario depends on how comfortable we are with ourselves. If we expect too much of either ourselves or the situation we find ourselves in, we are likely to lose our sense of contentment and start to become stressed. A realistic appraisal of oneself and one's situation can greatly increase personal contentment and reduce the risk of chronic stress.

SOCIAL SUPPORT SYSTEMS are a critical component in the battle against toxic stress. If we have supportive relationships, with both family members and partners, we are likely to deal with stressful situations far more successfully. Therefore, how we handle severe stress will in part depend on how stable our social relationship networks are. Social support systems seem to act as an emotional buffer zone between us and the stressor in question. While perhaps not eliminating the stress experienced, these relationships certainly help us cope with the stressor in question.

OPTIMUM STRESS LEVEL is an important concept when dealing with stress. The brain requires a certain minimum level of daily stress to function properly. Stress therapists feel that we need to raise our stress levels to a moderate level and try and keep them there. Too much or too little stress reduces our ability to cope with life. Keeping stress at an optimal level is a considerable challenge, but it is important for maintaining good mental health.

LACK OF GOALS is a concept that refers to stress arising from a perceived lack of purpose in life. It is particularly relevant for work-related stress. People in their middle years have often achieved goals they set out for themselves in life but have not created any new ones. As a result, they may begin to feel useless. They may float along aimlessly, losing their sense of contentment and becoming stressed in response to even minor problems. Women and to a lesser extent men, when reaching their late forties and early fifties, may experience 'empty nest' syndrome. After devoting much time to their children and making considerable sacrifices, they feel that a huge gap is left when their offspring leave home. Many no longer feel useful and struggle to carve out a future role for themselves. Such disillusionment and discontent can result in toxic stress, and alcohol is often used as a coping mechanism. Another at-risk group is those who retire – either due to age, redundancy or illness. These individuals may feel helpless, bored and apathetic. Having lost interest in life, they may become severely stressed. A commonly proposed solution to these scenarios is to set new goals or, as I would prefer to describe it, develop new passions.

Aimless 'floating' through life can be extremely destructive to our mental and physical health: we need to keep activating and challenging our minds to stay well. Passion for any activity or hobby 'switches on' our brain in a potent way, creating a protective environment that wards off toxic stress. If you find yourself 'floating' in this way, you need to recognise it and understand how damaging it can be to your mental and physical health. Then you need to open yourself to your inner passions and act on them. Many have developed a great sense of contentment upon discovering their creative skills and being courageous enough to embark on such a journey.

Using these concepts, we can learn new ways to find contentment in life, by setting realistic goals, discovering new interests, and keeping our stress levels at a constant but healthy level.

THE IMPORTANCE OF DIGNITY is perhaps one of the least-discussed topics in understanding how we as human beings cope with stress. With the industrial/technological revolution of the past two hundred years, in many cases the place of the human being has been downgraded. We are often seen as mere 'economic units', of little worth in ourselves.

Thus, our job can often come to define who we are – and so, if we lose our job, we often lose ourselves! The shame associated with no longer being a functioning economic unit when we are without work can bring on very high levels of toxic stress. We forget that we are fathers, mothers, sons, daughters, neighbours and friends, and need to fully appreciate our importance to all of the people around us. Our real dignity lies not in what we 'do' but rather in who we are as people: special and unique. If we can introduce this concept into our daily lives, the protective effect is enormous. This is the underlying principle behind the Raggy Doll Club – which we will be looking at later in the book.

Stress and the Developing Child

One area increasingly coming under scrutiny is the role of stress in the developing child. For a child to develop normally, he or she needs to be somewhat exposed to the harsh realities of life, and to learn that life is not always fair, and that we cannot always have what we want. Parents sometimes try to shield their children from the difficulties of life: such overprotective behaviour puts the child at an increased risk of chronic stress when they are later exposed to life's challenges, as they will inevitably be. At the same time, exposing children to stress above and beyond what they can cope with will hype up their stress system, with long-term negative consequences. This is most often observed in children reared in abusive or addictive environments.

The word 'resilience' is the term we use to describe our individual capacity to cope with stress. We now realize from research dealt with in my earlier books that children's brains are incredibly susceptible to stress during the key developemental stages from birth onwards. High glucocortisol levels can be very damaging to the immature developing brain. In extreme abuse situations children may end up with actual structural changes which predispose them to major depression later in life. We also know that some of those who lack resilience are far more likely to suffer from significant anxiety, will handle stress poorly as adults and are also unfortunately more at risk of self-harm.

Parents are nowadays being bombarded with so much 'psychobabble' (some of which comes from pop psychology and some well meaning advice from properly qualified experts) that it is proving difficult for them to trust their instinctive nature and allow the child to feel stress and discomfort in a monitored, healthy manner. We need to encourage resilience in young people, so that they can develop healthy stress systems to help them cope with the extremely complex world in which they find themselves.

Toxic Stress: The Role of Personality

The links between stress and personality have been under scrutiny for more than fifty years, with attempts to match particular personality types with harmful stress. But defining personality itself has proved difficult. The modern view is that, from a relatively early age, we all begin to exhibit particular *traits* which determine how we view things that occur in our lives – and that this in turn determines our behaviour. This behaviour is often regarded as the primary determinant of our personality type. We all develop our personality through a complex interaction between genes and our environment (*epigenetics*), which regulates the expression of these genes. Research into stress has identified four personality types:

TYPE A PERSONALITY is associated with those who are competitive, aggressive, impulsive, impatient and goal-orientated, and put themselves and those around them under considerable pressure to deliver targets. These people often take part in sports in order to achieve and may also engage in dangerous or unhealthy behaviours like driving aggressively, drinking and smoking. This aggressive, hostile behaviour is associated with an increased risk of developing coronary heart disease, due to the release of high levels of noradrenalin and glucocortisol and unhealthy behavioural patterns. Men seem to be more at risk of stress if they have this personality type – perhaps because they are more likely to be aggressive and angry in their behavioural responses to stress.

TYPE B PERSONALITY lies at the other end of the scale. It is associated with people who are less goal-orientated, calmer in response to problems, less aggressive and impulsive, and less likely to engage in the unhealthy behaviours described above. This group handles stress well and as a result are less inclined to suffer the symptoms of toxic stress.

TYPE C PERSONALITY is associated with people who are extremely passive and unassertive. They find it difficult to express their emotions, feelings or needs to others. People with type C personalities have been described as extremely cooperative, patient and accepting. They seldom display either anger or excitement and will rigidly control their facial expressions; they are usually highly introverted. These individuals suppress their feelings and do not stand up for themselves; as a result, they suffer more from stress and depression than any other personality type. Their immune system may end up attacking their own body. Their responses to stress also seem to increase their risk of developing and coping with certain types of cancer, such as malignant melanomas which grow on the skin (Temoshok et al 1987), and some forms of breast cancer, but the evidence for this is not completely conclusive! One of the functions of the immune system is to constantly monitor our body for cancer cells and kill them; perhaps the response of this group to stress may be compromising this process.

TYPE D PERSONALITY is associated with those who experience intense emotional distress, in social situations for example, but whose response is to lock it up inside themselves. They can be described as gloomy, anxious and socially inept. Type D behaviour is characterised by a tendency to avoid social contact with others. There is evidence that type D personality is associated with depressive and anxiety symptoms, post-traumatic stress disorder, social phobia and panic disorder. As is the case with type A personalities, when exposed to stress, this group is more at risk of heart disease due to the excessive release of noradrenalin and glucocortisol. High glucocortisol levels in particular predispose this group to an increased risk of heart disease.

*

Toxic stress is likely to be present where behaviour becomes extremely unhealthy. It is not any particular personality type which causes problems, but rather the person's response to stress which results in a predisposition to heart disease and cancer. Simply possessing some of the traits mentioned above does not necessarily mean that a particular person will experience significant risks to their health. Furthermore, other protective influences in our lives may shield us from these dangers. However, if any of the above personality trait descriptions seem to apply to you, it may be important for you to begin tackling stress.

Although personality itself is relatively stable over a person's life, it is possible to reshape patterns of thinking and behaviour and thus reduce the risk of toxic stress. Our brain has the capacity to change to facilitate this.

The Deadly Links between
Stress and Suicide

Each year, more than fifty thousand people will self-harm in Ireland and between four hundred and six hundred will die by suicide. Stress is linked with these incidents to an increasing extent. The reason for this lies in the links between the individual's stress system and their brain. Depression can be triggered by chronic stress, and experiencing unhealthy stress as we are growing up results in changes in the brain which can predispose us to this illness. Post-mortem studies on victims of suicide have shown that the stress system has been activated for some time before death. These studies have found that the adrenal stress gland was increased in size, and that there were high levels of glucocortisol and stress peptides in the brain and body prior to suicide. This has been observed in a variety of mental-health problems, including depression, addiction, schizophrenia and personality disorder. In each case, stress seems to be triggering thoughts of self-harm and associated behaviours.

Responses to toxic stress often involve excessive alcohol consumption. This dramatically increases the risk of suicide, as alcohol prevents the logical brain from controlling impulsive thoughts and behaviour.

But why is toxic stress such a risk in relation to suicide? We know that all of us have a logical and an emotional brain. When we are emotionally well, the logical brain is able to keep the emotional brain 'in check'. Most mental illnesses relating to anxiety and depression occur due to a breakdown in this control mechanism. When we become significantly stressed, high glucocortisol levels, along with high stress peptide levels in the brain, tend to weaken and damage the crucial pathways between the emotional and the logical brain. In depression in particular, the logical brain's control over self-harm thoughts and behaviour may be compromised. Those who would like to read more about these links should see my book, *Flagging the Problem*.

There is a national sense of hopelessness and pessimism in Ireland at present – and this is leading, together with housing, unemployment, financial difficulties, and relationship breakdowns, to an epidemic of toxic stress. Our young men under the age of thirty-five, many of whom feel disconnected from society, are particularly vulnerable to depression and often turn to alcohol. Thoughts of self-harm may follow.

Unemployment can be a major contributor to stress, depression and suicide. Recent evidence from the Irish Suicidology Association shows a two- to three-fold increase in suicide in men, and up to a six-fold increase in women, where unemployment is a factor. While this was an issue during the Celtic Tiger years, since the recession began there have been increases in young male suicides. It is a particular problem for young men in this age group, as they are more likely to use alcohol to cope and to turn to potentially fatal methods of self-harm.

More and more family doctors and counsellors are seeing a typical at-risk group emerging in the post-Celtic Tiger era. This group often consists of unemployed young men, generally aged between twenty and twenty-seven. Some have not done the Leaving Cert, having left school before the construction industry collapsed; others have been in jobs which have dried up; still others have come through college and find themselves on the 'rubbish dump' of modern Irish society.

They feel ashamed when they are asked about what they are 'doing with themselves'; their self-esteem is usually down in their boots. They feel useless and often hopeless about the situation they find themselves in. Many have to live with their parents for financial reasons, and this creates all kinds of domestic difficulties. Many use alcohol to try to cope with the stress created by this situation.

The real difficulties may appear when they become involved in relationships, often at a very young age. If there are offspring, the situation often becomes more complex. Unfortunately, many of these relationships end up breaking down, often in an acrimonious manner – and with the father being denied access to the children.

In many cases, the stress and loss of self-esteem created by these typical scenarios may lead to the onset of major depression. If this happens, suicidal thoughts may begin to appear. If a relationship breakdown occurs following the other stress triggers, these thoughts may harden into more concrete plans for suicide. The result is often tragic – with families having to live the rest of their lives with the resultling burden of guilt and loss.

We know from research that men and women are hard-wired differently, and that this is probably the main reason why men in these age groups exhibit a much higher risk of suicide. We know from national suicide statistics that four times as many young men die by suicide than women in the same age groups. In general, men are hard-wired to 'talk to themselves' rather than to others when they get into such stressful situations. The debate over whether such behavioural patterns are due to environmental influences during our upbringing or genetic/hormonal factors continues. In practice, although both are important, it seems likely that what happens hormonally in the womb is key.

GPs are also seeing older men and women struggling with similar stressors, particularly relating to personal debts, and being overwhelmed by them. The typical pattern is that toxic stress triggers depression, and in some cases suicide. As we have already mentioned, men often do not reveal their distress and end up getting into major difficulties, sometimes tragically seeing suicide as the only way out.

I think we also underestimate the importance of the emotion of 'shame' when discussing older age groups, particularly the forty-five-to-sixty-five bracket. Some, when faced with the shame of bankruptcy and possible loss of their income, their home and, most important of all, their self-esteem, may become overwhelmed, and see suicide as the only way out of the mire! There have been some very high-profile men who fit this pattern (e.g. Robert Maxwell).

Teaching people to identify and deal with chronic stress could reduce the chance that they will end up in these types of situations, and may potentially save lives. Redefining our interpretation of stressors can transform how we deal with stress. But to seriously challenge the carnage that chronic stress, leading to depression and suicide, is creating within our society is going to require a national change of policy. We need to learn from countries like Scotland (where they have absorbed all interested in suicide prevention under one organized, funded body) that have managed to create such a policy. Australia, for example, has reduced the risk of suicide by 25 percent. A great deal has been done in Australia in particular to reduce the stigma of depression in men through well organized media campaigns helping them to open up about emotional difficulties and seek help from professionals.

Above all, we need to create a safe environment for people experiencing toxic stress – whether it is through face-to-face consultations, telephone helplines, or monitored websites, internet chatrooms and bulletin boards. Groups like Aware, Console and the Samaritans are leading the way in reaching at-risk groups and providing the assistance which these people need in order to stay safe.

Toxic Stress: A Holistic Approach

A therapeutic solution to toxic stress should follow a holistic approach (see Figure 5). The various components of this approach in relation to stress are outlined below; for those interested in learning more, all the therapies are dealt with in detail in *Flagging the Therapy*.

EMPATHY The ability to sense another person's emotional state can be a powerful healing tool. Most people innately possess this capacity. When choosing a health professional to help you deal with your distress, you must feel there is some sort of 'meeting of minds'. You should feel comfortable about opening up to this person before entering into a therapeutic relationship with them. Some of us will be able to deal with chronic stress without feeling the need to work with a counsellor or therapist, but many will find the empathic bond which results from therapy helpful.

LIFESTYLE This plays a major role in the treatment and pre-vention of chronic stress. Research continues to emphasise the

importance of exercise. What form of exercise is most beneficial, how often, and for how long, are questions exercising top
research minds. The general consensus is as follows:

- Thirty minutes of brisk exercise, preferably three to
  five times a week, is ideal;
- Longer periods of exercise do not confer extra benefits;
- Any form of exercise – walking, jogging, weightlifting,
  swimming – is equally effective;
- Creative exercise, like dancing and water aerobics, are
  also effective and have the benefit of an extra social
  dimension;
- Staying close to nature (visiting forests, lakes and
  seascapes) is often overlooked in relation to preventing
  and treating toxic stress; combining this with exercise
  offers us the benefits of both!

Diet is also important, as the brain is dependant on proper
nutrition to function. A balanced diet when we are stressed can
improve how we feel. I recommend the following:

- A sensible mix of fresh fish (particularly oily fish like
  salmon, mackerel and tuna), eggs (especially free-
  range), meat, vegetables, cereals, nuts, flax seeds and
  oils, grains and fruit;
- Prepare your own food, and avoid fast food and
  highly processed foods as much as possible
- Eat, even when you are extremely stressed, as the brain
  cannot run without fuel;
- Avoid high-stimulant drinks like coffee and Coke,
  which many with stress and anxiety use in abundance;

- Avoid high-sugar 'hits', as fluctuating blood-sugar levels do not help good brain functioning;

- Avoid the 'extreme diets' sometimes recommended by alternative 'experts', which often exclude key foods;

- Avoid using food as a 'crutch' when feeling stressed or anxious;

- The main supplements believed to promote mental health are OMEGA 3 FISH OILS, and the key B vitamins folic acid, B6 and B12. All of these have been extensively investigated and there is substantial evidence to support their use as part of a holistic approach to stress. I recommend a B-complex supplement daily and Omega 3 oils (particularly EPA), in a daily dose of 500-1000 mgs;

- Pay special attention to the diet of young people (who are increasingly exposed to the ravages of toxic stress), which is often high in quantity and low in quality, at a critical stage of brain development.

ALTERNATIVE THERAPIES From the range of alternative therapies on offer, relaxation exercises, yoga, pilates and mindfulness are of proven benefit in treating toxic stress. Let's take a brief look at some of these therapies. What is very appealing to many people is the fact that these are natural therapies and often make us 'feel better' about ourselves.

MEDITATION is a mental technique which involves focusing the mind on an object, sound, prayer, breathing, or conscious thought, in order to increase our awareness of the present moment, helping us to relax, reduce stress or enhance spiritual or personal growth. Of the alternative/complementary therapies on offer, this is the most interesting. It is a therapy with a sound scientific basis which has helped us understand the workings of the mind/brain in a different way. I have no hesitation in recommending it to all who suffer from stress.

In mental health, we have benefited from excellent research by Prof. Richard Davidson, who has examined what happens in the brain as a result of regular meditation. Because of his work, we now know that meditation shifts activity from the right side of the brain (the source of most of our negative thoughts and emotions) to the left. This explains the reduction in stress, increase in positive emotions like peacefulness, calmness, forgiveness, love, compassion and joy, reduction in negative thinking, and so on.

The practice of mindfulness is particularly worthwhile. Mindfulness is a form of meditation where we focus our mind on the present moment and are aware of our thoughts, emotions and body in the here and now, without passing judgement on ourselves. It has been shown to be a powerful tool in reducing the effects of toxic stress; it helps combat anxiety and depression, and even strengthens our immune system.

I often recommend the following simple 'Three-minute Breathing Space' exercise, and encourage you to build it into your everyday life. It can be done at any time of the day, and is particularly useful if you are under stress. It involves finding a quiet space for three minutes, adopting a comfortable posture and closing your eyes. Then you should do the following:

MINUTE 1: Focus your mind on inner experiences, your thoughts, emotions and physical sensations. Do not try to change or challenge them, just become aware of them.

MINUTE 2: Focus on the physical sensation of breathing, on the rise and fall of your chest with each breath. Again, do not try to control your breathing.

MINUTE 3: Become increasingly aware of your whole body, your posture, your facial expression and your bodily sensations. Accept how you are feeling without judgement.

YOGA This is an ancient Indian therapy which combines physical exercises, meditation and breathing techniques. The word itself means 'union', referring to the union of mind, body and spirit which has its base in ancient Hinduism. The combination of physical and breathing exercises can be used to reach meditative states. In the West, it is considered a form of physical exercise by many, but the relaxation/breathing exercises/meditation side of this therapy can be useful as a complementary therapy in stress. The main type of yoga used in the West is hatha yoga; it is based on bodily postures called 'Asanas', breathing exercises called 'Pranayama', and meditation.

AROMATHERAPY A therapy with roots in the ancient Persian, Greek and Roman eras. It is a 'scent-using therapy', with essential oils extracted from plants (leaves, flowers, roots, berries, and so on) being applied by massage, inhalation, or released into the atmosphere, with a view to treating various conditions. The theory behind this therapy is simple: the oils involved (absorbed through either the nose or the skin) arrive in the brain and have an effect on our stress system and mood. There is some evidence that aromatherapy acts as a 'relaxant', relieving symptoms of short-term stress.

MASSAGE This is a popular therapy whose roots go back to ancient China, Egypt, Greece and Rome. There are a number of differing approaches, involving touching or kneading the skin, with a view to reducing pain, stress and anxiety.

AROMATHERAPY MASSAGE involves a combination of massage with aromatherapy oils, which we discussed earlier.

SHIATSU is a Japanese massage therapy, strongly influenced by Traditional Chinese Medicine, involving the use of hands (fingers/thumbs/palms), feet, knees, elbow, and so on, to massage various 'life energy' acupressure points. It is probably no more effective than simple massage.

INDIAN HEAD MASSAGE is another popular therapy, with its origins in Ayurvedic Traditional Medicine. It involves massaging the scalp, neck, face, ears and shoulders, to induce a profound state of relaxation.

REFLEXOLOGY involves applying finger/thumb pressure to the soles of the feet, which are thought to be connected to different parts of the body through the nervous system. The concept that particular pressure points on the foot correspond to various parts of the body and can be used to diagnose illnesses has been scientifically disproved. In practice, it is much more likely that the biological effects of massage in general are the reason for any success achieved by reflexology in reducing stress.

The role of spirituality and religion in acting as a bulwark against toxic stress is often overlooked. Many people find that time spent in contemplation is both rejuvenating and stress-reducing.

We need to pay particular attention to the importance of sleep in the treatment of toxic stress. Sleep is vital for our physical and mental health: we all need approximately eight hours of sleep a night. When we are stressed, we struggle to sleep – even though we may feel exhausted. To improve our chance of a good night's sleep, the following advice may be helpful:

- Try to go to bed at a consistent hour – preferably before midnight;
- Try and exercise for thirty minutes a day;
- Avoid stimulants like tea and coffee;
- Be wary of using alcohol as an aid to sleep – this may lead to misuse and abuse;
- Avoid reading for any period in bed – unless the book is boring!
- Avoid watching TV or a DVD just before going to bed;
- Do yoga/mindfulness exercises before going to bed;
- If taking a midday nap, keep it to ten minutes or less;
- Try to sleep in an airy, well-ventilated room;
- Think about taking melatonin supplements;
- If problems persist, see your family doctor;
- Remember that major sleep difficulties can be a warning sign of depression as well as chronic stress.

Any holistic package designed to deal with stress must involve reviewing stress factors in our lives and being honest with ourselves and those around us. We must not be afraid to make major changes in employment, relationships, and financial matters. These issues will be examined in more detail later.

DRUG THERAPY is of limited benefit in chronic stress, unless the person has also developed depression, in which case it can be extremely effective. Tranquillizers are not recommended, as they carry a risk of addiction.

TALK THERAPY is, along with lifestyle changes, the therapy of choice for the management of toxic stress. For those who are experiencing stress, talk therapy can be an extremely good way of dealing with underlying problems.

Talk therapy, often called 'psychotherapy', is a means of treating psychological or emotional problems through verbal and non-verbal communication. It involves talking with a specially trained therapist and learning new ways of coping with distress. The immediate goal is to help the person increase their self-knowledge and their awareness of their relationships with others.

Psychotherapy helps people become more aware of their unconscious thoughts, feelings and motives. Its long-term goal is to make it possible to exchange destructive patterns of behaviour for healthier, more successful ones. There are many different forms of talk therapy, including counselling, psychoanalytic psychotherapy, cognitive behaviour therapy, behaviour therapy, interpersonal therapy, supportive psychotherapy, brief dynamic psychotherapy, and family therapy.

*

All of these have a place in the management of toxic stress, but two stand out: cognitive behaviour therapy and counselling in all its forms. We will be demonstrating the value of the former in the second part of this book.

Now that we have a deeper understanding of toxic stress and its effects, let's move on to a new SEVEN-STEP APPROACH to dealing with this potentially lethal condition.

Part Two

This section will introduce a simple seven-step programme which aims to help us recognise and deal with toxic stress. This approach, which is based on the concept of self-sufficiency, involves understanding how stress affects us personally, and developing techniques to deal with it. I will outline many common examples of everyday stress in the hope that the reader may identify with them and find them useful.

Dr Bill, the Stress-buster

In the following examples, our health professional demonstrating how to deal with a range of stressful situations will be 'Dr Bill'. Dr Bill specialises in stress management and its effects on mental and physical health. He suggests cognitive and behavioural changes which aim to help his patients deal more effectively with stress. He will be using simple CBT concepts – in particular the 'ABC' approach discussed above. His overall approach is based on a realistic appraisal of the person's situation, and he employs holistic solutions to 'detoxify' stress.

To benefit significantly from the seven-step program, you must be honest with yourself and accept that serious changes in many aspects of your life may be required. Changing the brain for the better requires significant changes to a person's behaviour. If you are not prepared to tackle key issues, you will struggle to deal with toxic stress. On the other hand, if you are prepared to put the effort in, you will experience profound benefits to your physical and psychological well-being.

Step One

Identifying Toxic Stress

For some, the first wake-up call that stress is a problem will involve ending up in a hospital following a heart attack! For others, it may involve succumbing to a significant viral infection or debilitating mental illness such as depression. We often ignore obvious warning signs, as heeding them will require serious changes in our lives. The first step in our programme is learning to recognise these warning signs. These signs can be divided into the following categories:

- Physical symptoms
- Psychological symptoms
- Unhealthy behaviours

PHYSICAL SYMPTOMS:

- Difficulty sleeping, waking up throughout the night, grinding teeth when asleep, and having nightmares
- Persistent tension headaches
- Abdominal symptoms such as constipation, diarrhoea, stomach pains and cramps

- Symptoms of anxiety such as sweating, palpitations, shortness of breath and deep sighing
- Muscle tension and muscle pain
- Bouts of viral and bacterial illnesses
- Loss of libido
- Obesity or weight loss
- Restlessness

PSYCHOLOGICAL SYMPTOMS:

- Chronic fatigue or exhaustion, often mistaken for physical fatigue
- Frustration, anger and intolerance
- Anxiety
- Feelings of hopelessness, worthlessness and helplessness
- Depression, and negative and suicidal thoughts
- Fixed ways of thinking, which can create problems at home and at work
- Poor decision-making
- Addiction
- Impaired short-term memory

UNHEALTHY BEHAVIOURS:

- Smoking and excessive alcohol consumption
- Inactivity
- Not eating properly
- Use of stimulants such as caffeine or energy drinks to combat fatigue
- Using drugs such as hash or cocaine, or becoming addicted to prescription medication

- Staying up late at night
- Spending too much time on inappropriate internet sites – many of which may not be helpful
- Constant negative rumination on the problems facing us

If any of these symptoms or behaviours applies to you, take out a pen and paper and write them down. Identifying these symptoms is the first step towards recovery. The next step involves ruling out physical and psychological illnesses which may account for the distress. A visit to the family doctor may be necessary to complete this step. Your doctor may order a blood test, which can be helpful in two ways. First, you may suffer from a common condition which explains your symptoms. Secondly, if you are suffering from toxic stress, it may detect physical consequences arising from it.

The following conditions are easily diagnosed with a blood test, and should be ruled out before diagnosing stress:

ANAEMIA, resulting from iron deficiency. This is more common in women (usually due to heavy periods) than men

DIABETES, which may present with fatigue, thirst, and abdominal pains

THYROID DISEASE, where an underactive thyroid may result in weight loss, tremors, fatigue and feeling too hot. An overactive thyroid may result in weight gain, feeling cold, sluggishness, fatigue, coarse dry skin and hair loss.

Two psychological conditions often confused with chronic stress are generalised anxiety disorder and depression (major depressive disorder).

GENERALISED ANXIETY DISORDER (GAD) can present with some or all of these symptoms:

- intense anxiety and foreboding
- excessive worry about health, family or job issues
- a constant sense of impending disaster
- mental or physical fatigue
- impaired memory and concentration
- muscle tension, restlessness and tremors
- sleep difficulties, nightmares and teeth grinding
- indecisiveness, avoiding new situations or starting new tasks
- irritable bowel symptoms, tension headaches, sighing and palpitations
- loss of appetite and weight loss or weight gain

MAJOR DEPRESSIVE DISORDER (MDD) can present with some or all of the following symptoms:

- extreme low mood for a period of more than two weeks
- extreme fatigue – usually much more severe than in GAD
- anxiety
- weight loss or weight gain
- poor concentration and poor short-term memory
- loss of self-esteem
- reduced drive and libido
- loss of pleasure
- sleep difficulties – particularly early-morning wakening

- negative thoughts about ourselves, those close to us and the world in general – the typical ones being 'I'm worthless' and 'The world would be better off without me', and
- suicidal thoughts, plans or actions.

It is obvious that chronic stress, generalised anxiety disorder and depression share certain symptoms. So how can you tell them apart?

Depression is the simplest disorder to identify. Symptoms such as severe and persistent drops in mood, energy levels, concentration, drive, sleep and appetite are much more pronounced than in the other conditions. Most people suffering from chronic stress are able to get on with their lives, but those with depression may struggle to cope. Chronic stress is now recognised as a precursor to depression. What differentiates the two conditions are the severity of symptoms in those who are depressed, and a lack of any obvious trigger in depression.

It is more difficult to separate GAD from chronic stress, as the symptoms are remarkably similar. Many therapists feel that stress and anxiety are two sides of the same coin. However, chronic stress usually has a clear, identifiable cause, whereas those suffering from GAD will have a history of worrying, foreboding and fearfulness, without any obvious trigger. One can usually associate chronic stress with particular events and stressors.

As all three conditions result in increased levels of glucocortisol, their negative consequences on physical and psychological well-being are similar. The treatments for the three conditions differ, though, so accurate diagnosis is of paramount importance. Let's look at a few examples.

'I just feel so tired'

Mary is thirty-one and struggles with looking after three small children and working part-time in a busy office. She comes to see Dr Bill complaining of constant fatigue over the previous three months. 'There has to be something physically wrong with me,' she says. 'It's not normal to feel like this.'

On further questioning, she reveals a host of other symptoms. She is sleeping poorly, suffering from nightmares and waking with jaw pain each morning. She feels irritable and on edge, and has lost weight. She also notes that her concentration at work has waned: she has been pulled up on a number of occasions over errors she has made. This has only worsened her feelings. Her best friend was worried that she had become depressed and had persuaded her to visit Dr Bill. Mary was concerned herself because her mother had died in her fifties from a stroke. Her life is stressful: she is on the go from early morning and collapses into bed, exhausted, every night. She admits to drinking and smoking more than she used to. Her husband is doing his best to help, but she feels overwhelmed.

Dr Bill rules out depression and, although she has some symptoms of anxiety, decides that she does not meet the criteria for GAD. Further examination rules out obvious physical symptoms such as high blood pressure. A blood test indicates that she does not suffer from anaemia, diabetes or thyroid disease. He explains to Mary that she is exhibiting all the signs of chronic stress. Mary has now achieved the first objective, in that she has finally identified the cause of her fatigue.

'I have lost interest in everything'

Jim's wife encourages him to make an appointment with Dr Bill, as she has become increasingly concerned about his lack of interest in activities. There is a family history of diabetes, and although Jim is only forty, she has become convinced that this must be the underlying problem.

Like most men, Jim finds it difficult to talk about how he feels. However, he gradually begins to open up to Dr Bill about his various symptoms. He says he is constantly fatigued and on edge, is eating and drinking too much, and is tired no matter how much he sleeps. His libido has plummeted over the previous six months: he says he has 'no interest' in sex. He admits that he is often worried and finds it difficult to concentrate. He says he doesn't feel depressed but just 'not himself'. He finally blurts out that he has struggled with dealing with being put on part-time hours at work, saying: 'I just can't cope.'

After further examination and some blood tests, Dr Bill explains that Jim's loss of drive is not due to any physical illness. He warns him, however, that his eating patterns are predisposing him to this in the future due to his family history. Dr Bill excludes depression and explains that Jim is suffering from chronic stress brought on by fears that he will lose his job. Jim has begun the first part of the journey back to health: identifying the cause of his stress.

'I must have a brain tumour'

Sue presents to Dr Bill complaining of persistent headaches over the previous month. She is a twenty-seven-year-old secretary who works for a company that is struggling to survive the recession. She is convinced that the headaches have a sinister cause and breaks down in tears. She admits to being constantly fatigued, picking at her food, irritable with her partner, and with a constant feeling of butterflies in her stomach. She tosses and turns at night and is taking large quantities of painkillers.

She does not feel depressed but is not enjoying life as much as she used to. The headaches are starting to take over her life, and her concentration and memory are suffering. Her mother had suffered from chronic anxiety but Sue doesn't feel that she is an 'anxious person'. She admits that her workplace is a source of increasing stress for her and is concerned about the risks of the business folding.

Dr Bill checks that her blood pressure is normal. He rules out migraine and decides to refer her for a brain scan to eliminate any serious conditions, such as a tumour. All comes back clear. He then explains that her headaches are due to chronic stress and that eliminating this stress will involve tackling the underlying causes. Sue realises that her headaches do not have a sinister cause, but are the result of stress.

'I am constantly sick'

Matt arrives to see Dr Bill with a long list of low-grade infections. He has been experiencing cold sores, mouth ulcers, chest infections and stomach upsets. He is worried that there must be some serious underlying problem. On further questioning, he admits to constant fatigue, and that he has been drinking alcohol in large quantities. He has also been sleeping poorly and has had a lot of muscle pain and numerous low-grade headaches.

Matt is a mechanic; he is working longer hours due to the difficulties the motor industry is facing. He commutes long distances to work and is generally irritable and tired upon returning home. Following a thorough examination, Dr Bill sends Matt for blood tests. When the results return clear, Dr Bill explains that chronic stress is a common cause of the symptoms of which he is complaining. Matt was concerned about his family history of heart disease. Dr Bill explains that stress itself could increase his risk of heart disease and that he would have to make major changes to his life in order to deal with the problem. Matt has learnt how important it is to identify chronic stress in his life – which is the first step towards a return to health.

'My employer has sent me here!'

Tom's boss refers him to see Dr Bill. He is extremely put out by the fact that he has to attend as he is a 'very busy man'. His boss has sent him to the doctor because Tom had mentioned in passing that he was experiencing chest pains. Tom is an extremely successful businessman, but is renowned for having a very short fuse. In Tom's world, everything had to be done 'yesterday'. He felt that he was just wasting the doctor's time – and, more importantly, his own.

Dr Bill notes that Tom's father had suffered a major heart attack in his fifties but had survived it – only to die five years later from a massive stroke. On further questioning, Tom admits that he is smoking forty cigarettes a day and drinking significantly more alcohol than the recommended weekly limit. When the word 'stress' is mentioned, Tom starts laughing: 'I wouldn't know what the word means. That's for weaklings.' It becomes obvious he has a type A personality, and that his father probably had a similar disposition. Dr Bill is concerned about Tom's chest pains and notes that Tom's blood pressure is elevated and that his blood fats are very high. He decides to send Tom to a cardiologist, who puts three stents into his coronary arteries. Tom arrives back to Dr Bill a chastened man: the cardiologist has explained how close he was to a major, life-threatening event. Dr Bill goes on to explain the concept of toxic stress and the dangers of having a type A personality; he tells Tom that his lifestyle is putting his health at risk. At the root of Tom's problem lies his demand that the world must change to suit him – an approach which can be described as 'low frustration tolerance'. Tom also grasps that his unhealthy lifestyle is having an adverse impact on his health. Tom argues that he is too busy to change, but Dr Bill points out that the cemetery is full of very busy young men. This is the start of Tom's journey towards a new life.

'I just feel terrible!'

Monica comes to see Dr Bill but struggles to explain what is wrong with her. 'I just feel terrible!' she exclaims. She is a thirty-two-year-old mother of one. Both her partner and herself are working a three-day week. Money is tight – they are barely able to make the mortgage repayments – and they are both afraid of losing their jobs. She assumes that she is suffering from stress: she complains of feeling very down and exhausted, is struggling to eat, sleep or concentrate, and has lost all interest in life. Were it not for her three-year-old child, she would consider 'ending it all'. After saying this, she breaks down. She feels ashamed that she could even think like this, as she has a loving husband, a beautiful child, and is lucky to have a job. With Dr Bill's help, she soon realises that she is not suffering from stress, but from depression. It emerges that there is a history of depression: her mother had been hospitalised for severe postnatal depression. Monica had initially been experiencing stress, but after a pro-longed period had slowly slipped into depression. Her journey involves first dealing with her depression, and then later developing more effective ways of coping with stress.

'I am spending my day on the loo!'

Bob arrives to see Dr Bill in an exasperated state after a two-year battle with abdominal pains, cramps and alternating con-stipation and diarrhoea. 'It is taking over my life,' he explains. He is working in a busy insurance company and is under a lot of pressure there. He explains that 'results are everything' and reveals that, so far, five of his colleagues have been let go. He feels ashamed of his problem and is increasingly concerned about the possibility of cancer, as his father died of bowel cancer. Due to this family history, Dr Bill sends Bob for a colonoscopy; the results come back clear. Dr Bill explains the concept of chronic stress and how it is often related to anxiety. He explains that Bob's emotional brain was triggering his symptoms, as it controls the nerve supply to his bowel, resulting in persistent stimulation of the bowel. Bob's journey will involve an understanding of the way in which his desire for complete certainty in his life resulted in his bowel becoming overactive. He grasps that he needs to learn to understand how stress is impinging on his life and how to develop coping mechanisms to deal with it.

'I get so stressed'

James, a forty-four-year-old plumber, presents to Dr Bill complaining of feeling 'stressed all the time'. On further questioning, it turns out that he is a passive partner in a very manipulative marriage where his wife is very domineering. Throughout his life, he has failed to stand up for himself – both at work and at home. James's father had been of a similar disposition and had died in his fifties. Although James was concerned about this, he was more stressed about his unhealthy relationship. After discussing matters with Dr Bill, he discovered that his upbringing and personality had led him to be less assertive, resulting in toxic stress. Dr Bill explains that through assertiveness training and a lot of hard work, James would not only feel better about himself but would also improve his physical well-being. After using assertiveness techniques learned on a course, he faced up to people who had made his life a misery – including his wife – and they tended to back down.

'I find social situations stressful but just bottle it up'

Louise, a thirty-three-year-old executive, comes to see Dr Bill complaining of feeling stressed, particularly in social situations. She dreads attending social events, and relives her performance afterwards. 'I am like a cut-down version of my father,' she notes gloomily, 'and look how long he lasted.' It turns out that her father had also dreaded social situations, and had turned to alcohol to cope with them. He died of a massive heart attack at age sixty. Louise is smoking heavily and, like her father, drinks too much at social situations to cover up her feelings of social inadequacy. Of particular concern is her negative assessment of herself and her future as a result of the social difficulties she is experiencing. Dr Bill also wonders about type D personality traits, and the potential dangers associated with them. He shows her how simple CBT exercises can help her deal with her social anxiety and transform her life. He also advises her to change her lifestyle, in particular her smoking.

*

It is clear from the above examples that stress can present itself in varied forms and can threaten a person's physical health as well as their psychological well-being. If you can relate to any of the above stories, you have taken the important first step of recognising that stress is a problem for you. The second step – learning to identify the thoughts, emotions and behaviours underlying the chronic stress you are experiencing – is as simple as 'ABC', as we will see!

Step Two

Dealing with Our Thoughts, Emotions and Behaviour – The 'ABC' Model

The psychotherapist Albert Ellis transformed the way we deal with thoughts, emotions and behaviour by devising the 'ABC' model. This model is particularly useful when coping with stress. Let's start by defining our thoughts, emotions and behaviours.

THOUGHTS are best defined as 'the words, images, ideas, memories, beliefs and concepts that flow in and out of our conscious mind'. It is important to note the following:

- Just because a thought comes into our mind does not mean it is true;
- Thoughts rarely exist alone but usually arrive in a flow, one quickly following another, in what's known as a 'cascade effect';
- Sometimes we can get seemingly random 'automatic thoughts' passing through our mind at lightning

speed. It is very important to become aware of these thoughts;

- Thoughts can be visual, logical or emotional in nature;
- Thoughts influence emotions, which in turn influence behaviours;
- While there is a major emphasis on positive vs. negative thoughts when dealing with mental health, perhaps the concept of 'realistic thoughts' is more useful when dealing with stress.

EMOTIONS relate to how we feel, and last for relatively short durations, usually minutes or hours. If a particular emotion lasts for longer periods, i.e. hours to days, we call them moods. Some experts combine emotions and moods, calling them 'feelings'. I have always preferred to keep these separate, as it reduces confusion. The rich tapestry of life is created through our emotions, as a world without them would be grey and empty. Emotions can be categorised as follows:

POSITIVE EMOTIONS include joy, happiness, pleasure, love, awe, trust, contentment and peacefulness;

NEGATIVE EMOTIONS include anger, fear, guilt, shame, hurt, jealousy, emotional pain, sadness and loss;

HEALTHY EMOTIONS include grief and loss, sadness, disappointment, annoyance, frustration and irritation, regret and remorse;

UNHEALTHY EMOTIONS include anxiety, depression, anger, emotional pain, shame, guilt, jealousy, envy and hurt.

The following are some important characteristics of emotions:

- Emotions are associated with physical symptoms. Fear is associated with palpitations, dry mouth and shallow breathing. Depression is associated with tiredness and sleep and appetite problems;

- Emotions can be negative but not unhealthy. Anger, guilt, sadness and loss are normal, healthy emotions following the death of a loved one;

- Just because emotions are negative or unhealthy does not mean that the person experiencing them is distressed or unwell;

- Emotions heavily influence our behaviour. If we are sad, we may cry; if we are angry, we may become aggressive;

- The decisions we make in life are more influenced by emotions than logic;

- Modern therapists believe that suppressing emotions is unwise and recommend that we accept and embrace them;

- While a great deal of emphasis is placed on the role of negative emotions in illnesses like depression and anxiety, it is often forgotten how powerful positive emotions such as love, hope, joy, compassion, trust and forgiveness can be in our lives. We know about the power of positive thinking, but need to hear more about the power of positive emotions! This is especially relevant when dealing with stress;

- Many emotions ascribed to thoughts and events are sourced in unconscious emotional memory created during upbringing and adult life. These emotions may be triggered by internal or external events;

- Emotions and thoughts are interconnected. Many people assume that our emotions control our thoughts. At first glance, this seems to be true, but many emotional responses to situations are based on thoughts or beliefs. It is the *interaction* between thoughts and emotions which will determine our mental health and how we cope with stressors.

BEHAVIOUR is best defined as 'what we do' in response to events occurring in our internal or external environment. It can be influenced by both logic and emotion. The following are some important characteristics of behaviour:

- Behaviour can be healthy or unhealthy. Typical examples of unhealthy behaviour in depression are misuse of alcohol and self-harm. Typical examples of unhealthy behaviour in anxiety are misuse of tranquillizers, and avoidant or perfectionist behaviour. Violence is an example of unhealthy behaviour in response to anger;

- We can change behaviour even if we are struggling to change thoughts and emotions. Changing behaviour can be a powerful tool in treating anxiety and depression. A good example of this is encouraging those with depression to exercise – which in turn helps lift mood. We can't *think* our way into right being – but we can *act* our way into right thinking. This can also be applied to toxic stress;

- We can indirectly change behaviour by changing thoughts and emotions;

- Safety behaviour is a common coping strategy used by a person to prevent them experiencing a distressing emotion, such as those experiencing panic attacks using tranquillizers;

- Avoidant behaviour is another coping strategy; this includes avoiding public areas in phobia or avoiding exercise in depression. These behaviours are also observed in chronic stress.

Ellis's insight was that it is not what happens to us in life that upsets us and causes us grief, but rather how we *interpret* what happens. This interpretation arises from belief systems we develop over the course of our lives. These beliefs can often be compared to a virus we pick up without noticing it, and which then begins to spread through all areas of our lives.

Ellis also demonstrated that the resulting emotions we feel, and the physical symptoms which accompany them, have particular behavioural consequences. It is often the physical symptoms or negative behaviours arising from our emotions that encourage us to come for help. He developed a simple 'ABC' approach.

A stands for ACTIVATING EVENT. This starts a particular chain of thoughts, emotions and behaviour. It can refer to an external event, either existing or anticipated, or an internal one, such as a memory, mental image, particular thought or dream. A useful way of examining the activating event is to divide it into:

THE TRIGGER, which relates to the actual event which begins the process, and

THE INFERENCE we draw from this trigger; in other words, how we interpret the event which has occurred. In many cases, this involves assigning a 'danger' to the triggering event. We need to understand why this event is bothering us.

B stands for BELIEF, a term which encompasses our thoughts, the demands we place on ourselves and our world, our attitudes, and the meaning we attach to internal and external events in our lives. We interpret the trigger described above through these beliefs. Ellis divided these beliefs into two groups: rational and irrational.

These were described as follows by a fellow colleague of mine, Dr Paul Gannon, an Irish GP who specialises in occupational medicine:

> RATIONAL BELIEFS (in relation to ourselves, others or the world in general) are those which lead to healthy negative emotions like anger, concern and sadness. These beliefs are self-limiting, problem-solving and empowering. They are a result of the person adopting a non-demanding philosophy and help us adapt to life events;

> IRRATIONAL BELIEFS (in relation to ourselves, others or the world in general) are those that lead to unhealthy negative emotions like rage, anxiety and depression. They are self-defeating, problem-generating and disabling, and impair our ability to cope.

C stands for CONSEQUENCES, which represents the emotional and behavioural responses which arise from 'A' and 'B' above. An example of this would be Joe, who is due to sit his driving test in two days' time. He becomes very stressed and anxious. If we were carrying out an 'ABC' analysis of his problem, it would look like this:

A. (Activating Event):

Trigger: His upcoming test.
Inference/danger: He might not pass his test.

B. (Belief/Demands):

- He must pass his test;
- If he doesn't, he will be a failure.

C. (Consequences):

Emotion: Anxiety.
Physical reactions: His stomach is in knots; he has a tension headache and is sighing constantly.
Behaviour – Joe:

- stops eating, as his stomach is upset, and
- wonders if he should find an excuse to cancel the test.

Another simple example of this would be when Sara finds out that a work colleague is about to lose her job. In this case, her 'ABC' would look like this:

A. (Activating Event):

Trigger: Her work colleague being let go
Inference/Danger: The thought that she might be next to lose her job

B. (Belief/Demands):

- She must be completely certain that she will not be fired;
- If she is fired, she won't be able to cope with being unemployed.

C. (Consequences):

Emotion: Anxiety
Physical reactions: Her stomach is in knots; she has a tension headache and is sighing constantly
Behaviour – Sara:

- stops eating, as her stomach is upset

- tries excessively hard to please her boss
- constantly rings a friend who works in personnel, seeking reassurance
- begins to look up future job options, and
- is constantly checking her finances.

Let's look at other common examples of chronic stress which present to Dr Bill, and how he uses the 'ABC' approach to tease out the problems.

'I feel trapped'

George is sent by the company doctor to see Dr Bill, as he was complaining of fatigue. He was falling behind in his work projects and had become increasingly irritable and snappy with work colleagues. He had been fully investigated physically, so Dr Bill decides to do an 'ABC' on the problem. They agree on the following:

A. (Activating Event):

Trigger: An increasing workload created by the retirement of two senior colleagues, with an embargo on new employees.

Inference/Danger:

- All responsibility was being passed on to him, doubling of his workload;
- He was 'trapped' in this situation, as jobs were very scarce;
- If he complained and was let go, he would not be able to look after his family.

B. (Belief/Demands): He must not lose his job.

C. (Consequences):

Emotion: Anxiety, chronic stress and low mood, and anger towards his employers.

Physical reactions: Fatigue, headaches and muscle tension.

Behaviour – George:

- muses constantly about losing his job
- tries excessively hard to complete his work projects perfectly
- becomes irritable with colleagues due to exhaustion and frustration
- sleeps poorly
- stops eating healthy food
- smokes more
- ceases to exercise, and
- starts looking for a new job.

'We will end up on the streets!'

Mary attends Dr Bill with a host of physical symptoms. After taking her history, conducting a physical exam and doing some tests, he quickly realises that she is suffering from chronic stress and anxiety. The stressor was a common one, namely housing. They decide to work together on an 'ABC' of the problem, which went as follows:

A. (Activating Event):

Trigger: She and her partner have fallen behind on their mortgage repayments and are receiving letters from the bank regarding their situation.

Inference/Danger:

- They may not be able to reach a compromise with the bank;
- As a result, they may end up in court and find themselves homeless.

B. (Belief/Demands): They must be able to meet their repayments.

89

C. (Consequences):

> *Emotions*: Anxiety, chronic stress and low mood.
> *Physical reactions*: Fatigue, headaches, muscle tension, weight loss due to lack of interest in food, and facial pain resulting from grinding teeth at night.
> *Behaviour* – Mary:
> - ruminates constantly on the fear of losing her house
> - ignores any new post in case it brings bad news
> - stops eating and can't sleep at night, and
> - rings her sister constantly looking for reassurance.

'I just can't concentrate!'

Peter, a student, is reaching the end of an intensive three-year PhD, but attends Dr Bill complaining of a lack of energy and concentration. This is a problem, as he has only three months to finish his thesis before his funding runs out. He has become convinced that some serious physical illness is underlying his symptoms and has come for a check-up. Following some tests, Dr Bill says that Peter's problems are caused by chronic stress. They apply the following 'ABC' to his situation:

A. (Activating Event):

> *Trigger*: Finishing his PhD.
> *Inference/Danger*:
> - He may not be able to complete his PhD properly and in time, and as a result may not succeed in obtaining the qualification;
> - His funding may run out before he can finish his thesis.

B. (Belief/Demands): He must complete his PhD within the timeframe allowed.

C. (Consequences):

Emotions: Anxiety, chronic stress.

Physical reactions: Fatigue, headaches, muscle tension, weight loss due to lack of interest in food, constantly feeling 'wired'.

Behaviour: Peter:

- ruminates constantly about what will happen if he is not awarded his PhD
- frets about what he will do if his funding runs out
- eats too much junk food
- procrastinates
- stops exercising
- drinks more alcohol, and
- smokes marijuana in an attempt to relax.

'I just can't go on!'

Joan comes to see Dr Bill at the end of a five-year period in which she has struggled to deal with her alcoholic husband, whose drinking has left the family facing financial ruin. She has only remained in the marriage for the sake of her two teenage girls, but the stress of the situation has worn her down, and a combination of physical and psychological symptoms have forced her to come for help. It becomes obvious that she has been suffering from chronic stress. To help her deal with the issue, Dr Bill does an 'ABC' of her problem:

A. (Activating Event):

Trigger: Living with an alcoholic husband.

Inference/Danger:

- Her husband is never going to change;
- She will be trapped in the situation because of her two children;

- At some point, she will cease to be able to cope with the situation.

B. (Belief/Demands):

- Her husband must change his behaviour;
- If he does not, she might have to consider leaving him.

C. (Consequences):

Emotions: Anxiety, chronic stress, anger and low mood.
Physical reactions: Fatigue, headaches, muscle tension, weight loss due to lack of interest in food.
Behaviour – Joan:

- thinks constantly about feeling trapped
- eats and sleeps poorly
- smokes
- stops exercising, and
- constantly fights with her husband over his drinking.

*

It is obvious from all of the above examples that the source of chronic stress lies in our interpretation of a stressor, and, as a result, the demands we place on ourselves and the situations in which we find ourselves. We can also see that it is usually the physical symptoms which arise from this stress that lead us to seek help, and that our behaviour often only makes matters worse. Managing toxic stress is not just about identifying our patterns of thought and behaviour; we must also learn to challenge these patterns. So let's move on to examining how we might do this.

Step Three

Challenging Our Interpretation of Stressors

We are all presented with a complex series of stressors through-out our lives. Often these stressors can be serious in nature, but our interpretations of what should be relatively innocuous stressors can lead us into just as much difficulty as the stressors themselves. The secret to understanding and dealing with toxic stress in our lives is to learn to logically evaluate stress triggers. One of the best ways of doing this is to visualise what will happen as a result of being exposed to this stressor. People have active imaginations, and a great capacity for concocting elaborate stories and mental images. However, just because we predict that a scenario will turn out a certain way does not mean that this will be the case.

Realising that these visualisations can give us a false impression of where we are now, or what will happen in the future, opens up a new way of thinking about – and dealing with – stressors. The problem is that we often develop set ways of thinking about things, which are difficult to challenge.

The good news is that, with commitment and hard work,

it is possible to 'mute' the negative stress responses to events in our lives. It is also important to note that everyone is different, and what is stressful for one person is not for another. People often find it difficult to grasp that other people do not get stressed in situations that might cause us great stress. The complex interaction between genes and the environment is different for each individual. Consider the following examples, involving five people who lose their job at the same company, but have different interpretations of this stressor.

'This is a disaster!'

Mary is devastated. Fortunately, she is only renting an apartment, but in her mind she already considers herself homeless. She anticipates that she will be unable to find another job, and so will not be able to pay her rent and will have to move out of her flat and return home to live with her parents. She predicts that she will be trapped in this situation for the foreseeable future. Her parents' home is fifty miles away from where she currently lives, and that will mean that her new boyfriend will definitely leave her. For her, losing her job is a disaster with which she will be unable to cope. While losing a job is stressful, Mary's *interpretation* of what will happen as a result is triggering chronic stress, despite the fact that she has no proof that these things will happen.

'How dare they fire me!'

John is furious. He is an ambitious businessman and believed that he was invaluable to the company. He considers himself much more able than some employees who were not let go. He reckons he will easily find another job; what bothers him is the insult of being fired. For John, the fear of unemployment is not a major stressor. However, the feeling that he has been mistreated could trigger a bout of stress over the coming months.

'This may present me with an opportunity!'

Peter, who works at management level, hears the news and is initially quite concerned about the potential consequences. He is married with two small children and has a mortgage to pay. But after the initial shock subsides, he begins to see an opportunity in the redundancy offer. He had been unhappy in his current situation for quite some time and had already begun to seek out contacts in the business world with a view to moving 'sideways'. Peter realises that he can pay off some of his mortgage with the redundancy money and begins to seek alternative employment. He has been able to interpret his job loss in a positive way, thereby neutralising the stressor.

'I am too old to find another job!'

Maura is devastated by the news. She is fifty, and her job is very important to her. It has helped her pay her bills, and provided her with a social network and a reason to get up every morning. But what is really bothering her about losing her job is her age: in her mind, she has no hope of finding work again, particularly in the current economic environment. She starts to visualise herself at home, alone, bored and unable to look after herself financially. In fact, Maura has no proof that her visualisation will come true, or that she will never be employed again. But she is so convinced that this will be the case that she slips into a bout of chronic stress and develops an alcohol addiction.

'We will lose the house!'

James feels as if his world has collapsed around him. He is happily married, with two kids just about to go to college, and still has a significant amount to pay on his mortgage. He is forty-seven and, like Maura, feels that his chances of getting another job are slim. But while he is concerned about his children and paying for their college education, his primary fear is that he and his wife will be unable to pay the mortgage on the house and that they will be forced to hand it back to the bank. He begins to create in his mind a nightmare scenario: the letters from the bank, the debt collectors at the house, the legal proceedings, and the pitying looks from family and friends. These thoughts overwhelm him. There is no doubt that for James, the stressor is indeed a significant one, but it is his visualisation of the consequences that result in toxic stress.

*

In all of the above cases, we can see that each person interprets the stressor of losing their job differently. Those who assess the situation logically have a reduced risk of becoming stressed. However, those who assign to the situation a consequence which may not actually materialise are likely to get into difficulty.

The best defence against chronic stress is to challenge your interpretation of a stressor. To do this, start by writing down the stressor on a sheet of paper, and attempt to answer the key

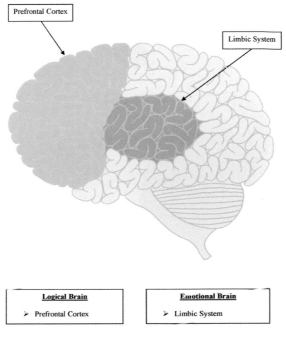

FIGURE 1: The Logical and Emotional Brain

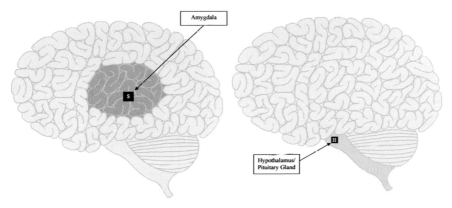

FIGURE 2: The Stress Box

FIGURE 3: The Horomone Control Box

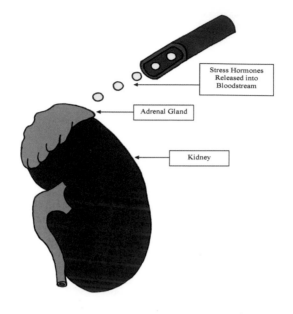

FIGURE 4: The Adrenal Gland

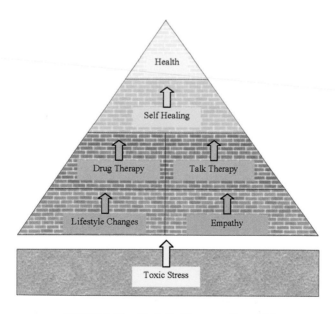

FIGURE 5: The Holistic Therapy Pyramid

ust

 wful

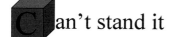 an't stand it

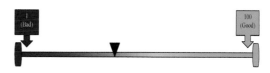

 elf Rating

FIGURE 6: The Big MACS   FIGURE 7: The Rating Scale

FIGURE 8: The Raggy Doll Club
(Based on the 1980s cartoon series *The Raggy Dolls*, created by
Melvyn Jacobson and produced for Yorkshire TV.
Adapted for therapeutic use by CBT Therapist Enda Murphy.)

A

Trigger

Inference/Danger

B

Beliefs/Demands

C

Consequences

Emotions

Physical Symptoms

Behaviours

FIGURE 9: The ABC Worksheet

question, 'Why is this bothering me at all?' The answer to this question usually results in a chain of similar questions: 'And why is that bothering me?', and so on Eventually, we find ourselves at the core of the problem. In the examples above:

- Mary's real 'danger' is that she will lose her boyfriend;
- Maura's 'danger' is that she is too old to get another job;
- James's 'danger' is that his family will lose their house and end up on the street.

To challenge a particular interpretation, we must fully understand it first. Once we have got to the root of the problem, we can begin to examine how accurate our interpretation is. Often, we have jumped to conclusions and made all kinds of assumptions that have no basis in reality. These narratives can take on a life of their own, and cause us to 'catastrophise' about what will happen to us. Tackling chronic stress is really about developing the skills to successfully challenge these irrational thoughts.

A light-hearted way of challenging the inaccurate interpretations we attach to stressors in our lives is to consider the following statement: 'People love to believe their own bull.' This means that we are adept not only at making up elaborate stories but also at convincing ourselves they are true!

To challenge this problem, we must attempt to prove that our visualisation is going to come true. This step involves brutal honesty, otherwise we will continue to fool ourselves and thwart our journey to recovery. More often than not, people realise that what they believe to be a real danger is in fact an imagined one.

For example, if Maura challenges her belief that she is too

old to get another job, she will realise that she has no evidence for this. She has never been in this situation before. She has not yet applied for any jobs, and not even considered seeking retraining. While getting a new job may be difficult, all the negative consequences she has anticipated may never arise.

Can James prove that his family will lose their home? Has he considered restructuring his mortgage repayments or using his redundancy money to ease the pressure?

John's approach to challenging his interpretation will be quite different from those of the others. He was most bothered about the fact that his employers could not see how important and valuable he was to the company. He was heading into a period of toxic stress as a result of his outrage and frustration at being let go. For John to challenge his interpretation, he must first work out what is really bothering him – that his employers did not appreciate him – and then be honest in challenging this. Was he really invaluable to the company? Did he fully understand the difficulties facing the company and what their restructuring plans involved? Could he prove whether his being let go made any significant difference? Or did John just 'believe his own bull'?

But what can we say to those who are presented with situations in which, no matter how we look at them, disaster seems to be lurking? Many who are in these situations are facing such a reality and can argue that no matter how they view the trigger facing them, it is impossible to find a 'silver lining'.

The reality is that challenging the 'A' in such situations is usually a waste of time. How can we say to a person with a young family about to be evicted by a heartless, uncaring financial institution, 'Don't worry, it will all work out for the best'? Or to say to somebody who has just been let go from a job and has little prospect of getting another one any time soon, 'Don't worry, things will work out – just stay positive'? Or to say to a hard-working self-employed person who has done everything in his power, including dipping into his hard-earned savings, to try to hold on to the jobs of the six people he is employing, 'Don't worry, just hang in there and everything will work out'?

For thousands of people in Ireland, these scenarios are a reality, and no amount of 'gloss' is going to change things. In such cases, challenging the validity of a stressor may seem pointless and almost an insult to their common sense. But we Irish are, as a people, incredibly resilient, and we have to come up with survival strategies for such situations. That is where challenging our underlying belief systems (particularly the ones which suggest we will not be able to cope or survive!) and the resulting negative behaviours will prove useful. A pragmatic or realistic approach can often make matters less stressful.

But there are many situations where the stressor is neither acute nor destructive. In these cases, it is our mental view of the potential problems that underlies our distress. With these provisos in mind, and having learned the importance of understanding and challenging our interpretation of stressors, let's examine the unhealthy beliefs and demands that often underlie them.

Step Four

Challenging Unhealthy
Beliefs and Demands

In the last section, we learnt that how we interpret events greatly influences how we deal with them. But what underlies the differences in the way each of us evaluates the stressors in question? How we interpret stressors and the resulting emotional and behavioural consequences depends greatly on our underlying beliefs, or the 'lens' through which we view life. These, as we have seen, include our thoughts and attitudes, the meaning we attach to internal and external events in our lives, and the demands on ourselves, the world and others. Most of us are unrealistic about the demands we make on ourselves, others and the world in general. These demands become problematic when they are not met. Just as we learned to evaluate and challenge our interpretation of stressors in the last section, we can also analyse:

- the role played by our personal belief system in analysing stressors

- the resulting demands we make of ourselves, and
- how to challenge these demands.

Only through understanding ourselves and how we think can we make serious changes to our lives and rid ourselves of chronic stress. Most cases of chronic stress centre on a particular scenario: a demand that things turn out a certain way, a perception that we will not be able to cope if they don't, and a period of being self-critical when and if this happens. We must learn to understand and challenge these unrealistic beliefs and demands. Dr Bill achieves this in the following examples:

'He just can't leave me!'

Sara has become extremely stressed, hurt and anxious following the sudden decision by her long-standing boyfriend, Ian, to leave her. She decides, after six months of hell, to visit Dr Bill. It is clear that she is struggling to come to terms with the situation; he decides to do an 'ABC' with her. Here we will deal only with the 'A' and 'B' that they agree on and see how she learns to challenge them.

A. *Trigger*: The breakdown of her relationship.
Inference/Danger:
- She will never again be able to find somebody she can love and trust to the same degree as she did Ian;
- As a result, she will end up alone.

B. *Belief/Demands*: They identify three unhealthy beliefs/ demands which are at the heart of Sara's distress and which are leading to most of her symptoms:
- Ian should not have left her;

- She must not be left alone, as she will not be able to cope (in my experience, this is one of the most common demands we make as human beings);
- She is a failure because she was unable to maintain the relationship.

Dr Bill moves on to show her how to challenge the above unhealthy beliefs and demands. He explains the 'Big MACS' (Figure 6), and how he and she will use them to challenge her demand. He then challenges her beliefs as follows:

M stands for MUST   Dr Bill explains that people who suffer from stress and anxiety live in the 'Land of Must', using absolute terms like 'ought', 'should' and 'must' to demand that things be a certain way.

He explains that when we talk about life in this way, we are really demanding one of four things: certainty, order, security or perfection. Sara realises that her demand that Ian should not have left her was an unrealistic and unfair demand. As Dr Bill explained, there was no law that stated that Ian – or indeed any partner – must stay in a relationship with her. She sought a level of control over his feelings and actions that was unhealthy and unrealistic. While it would have been preferable for her if Ian had agreed to stay in the relationship, there were many factors outside of her control – namely his feelings and plans for the future – which conflicted with their relationship. They agree that this demand was a burden on her, and that she would feel much better if she accepted his decision. Sara also realises that her demand for certainty that she never be left on her own is unreasonable and unhealthy – albeit understandable.

A stands for AWFUL Dr Bill goes on to explain that many people who suffer from stress and anxiety imagine the worst-case scenario, which is often catastrophic. They focus on the small chance that something will go wrong, rather than the more likely scenario that it won't. Sara immediately accepts this, admitting: 'I spend so much time worrying about all kinds of things that never come to fruition.' They agree that she has absolutely no proof that just because Ian left her, she would never meet anyone else and would definitely end up on her own.

C stands for CAN'T STAND IT This is common among those suffering from stress and anxiety. Sara doesn't think she can cope with being on her own. Dr Bill challenges this belief, pointing out that she has coped with far worse situations in her life.

S stands for SELF/OTHER RATING This lies at the root of stress, anxiety and indeed depression. It involves judging ourselves and taking on board the judgements of others. 'How would you have rated yourself before Ian left you, on a scale of one to a hundred,' Dr Bill asks. Sara replies that in general she would rate herself quite highly, probably around eighty. Her doctor draws a scale (Figure 7) and marks her rating on it. 'And where do you feel others would have rated you?' he asks. Sara replies: 'Around the same!' He added this to the scale. 'And since Ian left you, where would you rate yourself?' he asked. Sara replies that she would drop her rating down to ten. Dr Bill marks this in too. Dr Bill then asks: 'And how do you feel other people would rate you, because he left?' Sara says: 'About ten.'

'Now a more important question,' Dr Bill continues. 'Can we really rate a person?' On reflection, Sara agrees that we cannot do this, as we are too complex. He goes on to ask her if she would like to join a very special club, the 'Raggy Doll Club' (Figure 8). Intrigued, she asks him for more information.

He goes on to explain that this is a highly exclusive club, of which he himself has been a member for many years: 'But there are two important things members have to do in order to be allowed into the club: they cannot rate themselves, and they cannot accept other people's rating of us.'

He goes on to explain that the Raggy Doll Club was established by leading CBT therapist Enda Murphy and was loosely based on a TV cartoon series. The raggy dolls were the imperfect dolls which were left in the basket, and the series was about their adventures.

'So to join me in the Raggy Doll Club, you have to agree to accept these two criteria,' continues Dr Bill. 'The club is full of normal, fallible human beings who try to do their best. They don't always get things right, but they don't judge themselves harshly when they make a mistake, and they don't pay too much attention to the judgement of others. In the Raggy Doll Club, you accept yourself unconditionally.' Sara decides to join.

Dr Bill then summarises the progress they have made in challenging her beliefs/demands:

- She had been looking for complete certainty that Ian would not leave her. In practice, it is neither possible nor healthy to want to control another human being. So it was better to replace the word 'must' with 'prefer';

- This demand was a burden on her, and dropping it would help her feel better;
- She was seeking complete security in her life, and this is not possible;
- She had been imagining the worst in assuming that she would be left on her own, without any proof to confirm this;
- She assumed that she would not be able to cope on her own. In fact, she would learn to cope, even if this proved to be difficult;

She was criticising herself and assuming that others would do likewise, and would benefit from joining the Raggy Doll Club.

'She must get better!'

Sue has a particularly close relationship with her sister Maeve, who has developed breast cancer and subsequently struggled through surgery, radiotherapy and chemotherapy. Sue herself has become increasingly distressed, and begins to show all the symptoms of toxic stress. Her family encourages her to see Dr Bill. Together, they analyse the problem and come up with the following 'A' and 'B':

A. *Trigger*: Her sister's illness.
    Inference/Danger:
    - Maeve may die as a result of her illness;
    - If Maeve does die, Sue will not be able to cope.
B. *Belief/Demands*:
    - Maeve must not die.

Dr Bill convinces Sue that the best way to deal with her stress is to learn how to challenge this demand. He explains the concepts behind the 'Big MACS', and together they come up with the following:

MUST   He challenges Sue's need for complete certainty that Maeve will not die, as there was no such certainty in life. She could not control how her sister would react to a particular cancer. The variables involved, such as her sister's innate ability to fight cancer, the aggressiveness of the cancer itself, and her sister's reactions to the various therapies, were all out of Sue's control. It would of course be preferable if her sister were to survive, but *demanding* that she would survive is unrealistic.

AWFUL   Dr Bill challenges Sue's assumption that the worst will happen. In fact, Maeve might respond to treatment and make a full recovery.

CAN'T STAND IT   Dr Bill challenges Sue's belief that she would not be able to cope if her sister died. Although it would be painful and difficult, she would cope with it.

'She must stop picking on me!'

Pat is working in a large, impersonal organisation. Nine months previously, he had been reallocated to work in another department. His new boss, Pauline, seems to think that he was not suited to the department and she finds fault with every aspect of his work. He is finding the situation intolerable. He begins to demonstrate all the signs of chronic stress and eventually goes to see Dr Bill. They review the problem together and come up with the following 'A' and 'B':

A.   *Trigger*: His boss giving him unachievable deadlines and unmanageable workloads.

Inference/Danger:
- He is being picked on;
- He will eventually be fired.

B. *Belief/Demands*: They identify some key unhealthy beliefs/demands which are at the heart of Pat's distress and which are leading to most of his symptoms:
- He must make his boss like him;
- If she does not, he will not be able to cope;
- He must not lose his job;
- He is a failure because he doesn't stand up for himself.

Dr Bill encourages him to challenge these unhealthy demands. He explains the concept behind the 'Big MACS', and together they come up with the following:

MUST   Dr Bill challenges Pat's demand that his boss must like him. He has to appreciate that he cannot control the thoughts and behaviour of another person. Dr Bill also challenges Pat's demand for complete certainty that he would not lose his job. This is a particularly unreasonable demand in the current economic climate. While it would be better if his boss treated him with more respect, ultimately he could not control her.

AWFUL   Dr Bill challenges Pat's assumption that the worst would inevitably happen. For example, has he any proof that his boss is trying to get him fired?

CAN'T STAND IT   In particular, Dr Bill challenges Pat's belief that he would not be able to cope if his boss did not cease her harassment, or if he actually lost his job. He would find a way of coping – both for himself and for his family.

SELF/OTHER RATING   Finally, Dr Bill challenges Pat's statement that he is a failure and introduces him to the Raggy Doll Club, explaining that to become a member of the club he is not allowed to rate himself as a failure or indeed to accept his boss's rating of him as a person.

'I can't cope with his drinking!'

Anne has been highly stressed for the previous two years as she struggles to cope with her husband Joe's drinking. His drinking has increased significantly after he lost his job a year ago. In the beginning, she had assumed he was just trying to cope with his redundancy, but it became clear that he had become addicted to alcohol. She is at the end of her tether, with unpaid bills mounting up, constant arguments, and no obvious way out of her dilemma: the couple have a substantial mortgage in their joint names. Finally, her sister persuades her to go for help, and she arrives into the GP surgery to see Dr Bill. Dr Bill quickly identifies several warning signs of toxic stress; the fact that her mother died of cancer at a young age was of particular concern to him. Together with Anne, he examines the problem, and they come up with the following 'A' and 'B':

A.   *Trigger*: Joe's drinking patterns.
   Inference/Danger:
   - Joe's drinking was destroying her life;
   - They would end up losing their home if he did not stop;
   - He will eventually die from his addiction;
   - She will have a mental breakdown;

- She feels trapped, as separation is not financially viable for her.

B. *Belief/Demands*: They identify the unhealthy beliefs/demands which are at the heart of her distress and are leading to most of her symptoms:
- Her husband Joe must stop drinking;
- They must not lose their home;
- She is a failure because she cannot stop him drinking.

Dr Bill then encourages her to challenge these unhealthy demands. He explains the concepts behind the 'Big MACS', and together they come up with the following:

MUST   He challenges Anne's demand that her husband must stop drinking. She could not control this. While she considered Joe's drinking to be a problem for her, he would not change until it became a problem for him. It would be better if Joe stopped drinking, but it would take either ill health or financial ruin to bring him to his senses. Until then, matters are out of her control. He also advises her to attend Al-Anon, a self-help group where other spouses of alcoholics can help her develop an insight into how to deal with his drinking problem.

AWFUL   He challenges her assumption that the worst will inevitably happen. It is possible that they will lose their home because of how much money he spends on alcohol, but very few judges would throw a family out onto the street in such a situation.

CAN'T STAND IT   He challenges Anne's belief that she would not be able to cope if her husband does not stop drinking.

Although it would be difficult, she would still be able to cope.

SELF/OTHER RATING   Finally, he challenges her statement that she is a failure, and introduces her to the Raggy Doll Club. She reassures him that she is doing her best in a seemingly impossible situation.

'He must not take his own life!'

Joan has lived under a state of unrelenting stress as a result of her son Peter. Peter's best friend Mike took his own life two years previously. This has proven to be too much for Peter, who was let go from his apprenticeship at around the same time. He became withdrawn and refused to discuss either his own situation or his friend's death. Now everyone in the house lives in a constant state of apprehension that he will follow in his friend's footsteps.

Joan has always had a special relationship with Peter and is particularly stressed by his situation: she has lost weight and spends every waking minute checking on his whereabouts. This starts to wear her down. She eventually bows to family pressure and goes to see Dr Bill. He identifies that Joan is suffering from chronic stress and notes that there is a strong family history of depression: Joan's aunt took her own life due to depression. They review the problem and come up with the following 'A' and 'B':

A.   *Trigger*: The death by suicide of her son's best friend.
    Inference / Danger:
    • Peter is withdrawing from social life;
    • He has been seriously affected by the suicide of his best friend;

- He may have become depressed, and as a result may decide to take his own life.

B. *Belief/Demands*: They identify the following unhealthy beliefs and demands:

- Peter must not decide to take his own life;
- If he does commit suicide, she will not be able to cope and will be a complete failure.

Dr Bill encourages her to challenge these unhealthy demands. He explains the concepts behind the 'Big MACS', and together they come up with the following:

MUST   He challenges her demand that Peter must not take his own life. She cannot control his thoughts or behaviour. She should take some practical steps to get him the help he needs, but she can never be completely certain that events might not spiral out of control due to factors beyond her control. She has to accept that there will always be a slim chance that Peter will take his own life. If she does not accept this, she will be doomed to years of overwhelming anxiety.

AWFUL   He challenges her assumption that the worst would inevitably happen, and her visualisation of Peter in a coffin following such an incident. Was it not equally possible that her son might come for help? Did she have any proof that her visualisation would come true? If not, was she helping herself by spending days worrying about something that may never actually occur?

CAN'T STAND IT   He challenges her belief that she would not be able to cope if her son died by suicide. While it would be extremely difficult, she would cope with it, because of her responsibilities towards the other members of the family.

Self/other rating   Lastly, Dr Bill challenges her statement that she is a failure and introduces her to the Raggy Doll Club. Almost every mother and father who exists in the nightmare world of having a family member die by suicide rates themselves as absolute failures in the immediate aftermath of the death. This can lead to a lifetime of suffering. Unless they can become Raggy Dolls and accept that no matter what happens in life they can only do their best, this situation will not change. In relation to her son, all she can do in the current situation is 'hang on in there' with him. She cannot control what might happen and must accept that, no matter what actually happens, she has done her best.

'They must like me!'

David has become extremely stressed and anxious over the last year. His problems began when he started to date Delia, a girl from a very wealthy background. In the beginning, he was able to ignore the fact that her parents were extremely disapproving of the relationship, taking the view that he did not come from 'the right stock'. The situation came to a head when they got engaged and set a date for the wedding. Delia is now caught in a tug of war between her family and David. David himself has become stressed, as he began to feel that he is not good enough for her and worried that he was causing her distress because of her family's position. He feels trapped between his love for his fiancée and the pressure he feels to become someone he is not.

Due to the stress, his health deteriorates and he begins to consider breaking off the relationship. Finally, a major bout of shingles, triggered, he believes, by the stress, prompts him to visit Dr Bill, and they discuss the problem. Dr Bill treats his shingles but tells David that he will have to deal with his stress in order to avoid risking further health consequences. They discuss the situation and come up with the following 'A' and 'B':

A. *Trigger*: His engagement to Delia.
Inference/Danger:
- Delia's family considers David to be not 'good enough' for her;
- He feels inferior;
- He may end up coming between Delia and her family;
- Delia may side with her family and end the relationship.

B. *Belief/Demands*: They identify the following unhealthy beliefs and demands:
- Delia's family must accept him as being good enough for their daughter;
- Delia must not leave him;
- If they do reject him, he will feel that he is a complete failure.

Dr Bill encourages him to challenge these unhealthy demands. He explains the concepts behind the 'Big MACS', and together they come up with the following:

MUST He challenges David's demand that his new in-laws must accept him into their family and appreciate him. David needs to accept that he does not have this level of control over anyone. He also challenges David's demand for complete certainty that Delia not leave him if her parents do not accept him. It would of course be better if they stayed together, and he should do everything in his power to achieve this aim, but he has no right to insist on how another person feels or behaves.

AWFUL He challenges David's assumption that Delia will leave him by pointing out that David has no proof that this will in fact happen.

CAN'T STAND IT He challenges David's belief that he would not be able to cope if Delia left him. It would be difficult for him to cope, but he would manage because it would be in his own interests to do so.

SELF/OTHER RATING Finally, he challenges David's statement that he is a failure if Delia's family reject him, and introduces him to the Raggy Doll Club.

'I have to find the money!'

Bertha has been under persistent stress since she was put on a three-day week at work. She has always been a 'spend today, pay tomorrow' person and has reached the limit on her credit card. Her bank has issued her with a final warning, and the debt collectors are due to arrive within weeks. She is not sleeping or eating, is losing weight and is getting constant mouth ulcers as a result of the stress she is under. She is arguing with her boyfriend and continuously ringing up her best friend looking for advice. As her physical health begins to decline, those close to her convince her to attend Dr Bill for help. He is concerned about her physical health and initially recommends that she takes vitamin supplements, and gets thirty minutes of brisk exercise each day. Together, they come up with the following 'A' and 'B':

A. *Trigger*: The upcoming visit of the debt collectors.
Inference/Danger:
- She will not be able to come up with the money and will lose most of her possessions;
- Others close to her will find out that she is in debt;
- She will not be able to cope with the subsequent fallout.

B. *Belief/Demands*: They identify the following unhealthy beliefs and demands:
- Bertha must be able to find the money to pay off the debt collectors;
- She, and those around her, will think she is a complete failure.

Dr Bill encourages her to challenge these unhealthy demands. He explains the concepts behind the 'Big MACS', and together they come up with the following:

MUST He challenges her demand that she must be able to find the money to pay off her debts. She is looking for complete certainty that she will be able to pay them off, when in reality this is not possible. This is putting intolerable stress on her; she can only do her best. Perhaps she should consider attending MABS (the Money Advice and Budgeting Service), where she could seek advice on how to restructure her financial affairs. While her debts are a significant stressor in her life, it is not inevitable that disaster will follow!

Awful He challenges her assumption that the worst will inevitably happen: that all her valuables will be repossessed. She has no proof that this will happen.

Can't stand it He challenges Bertha's belief that she would not be able to cope if the debt collectors took all her possessions.

Self/other rating Finally, he challenges her statement that she is a failure and introduces her to the Raggy Doll Club. Dr Bill encourages her to make a distinction between her behaviour and who she is as a person.

'I have to get better!'

Paul has been extremely stressed for the previous year. He experienced major back problems following an accident and has been out of work ever since. As his debts began to mount and pressure from work increased, Paul was showing all the signs of toxic stress. His partner was aware that Paul has a family history of premature death due to heart disease, and became increasingly worried. She finally persuades him to go for help to deal with his stress issues. He goes to see Dr Bill and agrees that he is at risk physically and emotionally. Paul agrees to do some work on the issue, and together they come up with the following 'A' and 'B':

A. *Trigger*: Paul's back problems.
Inference/Danger:
- He is never going to get better;
- He will be let go from his job;

- He will be unable to find another job;
- He will be unable to look after his family financially;
- He dreads receiving letters from the bank;
- He could lose his house.

B. *Belief/Demands*: They identify the following unhealthy beliefs and demands:

- His back problem must get better;
- If he cannot get better and look after his family financially, he is a complete failure.

Dr Bill encourages him to challenge unhealthy demands. He explains the concepts behind the 'Big MACS', and together they come up with the following:

MUST   Dr Bill challenges Paul's demand that he must get better. Aside from doing what his specialist advised him to, he has no control over this. He was looking for complete certainty that he would get better, and this is not possible. He also had to accept that he was not responsible for the accident in question; rather, he had been the innocent victim of it.

AWFUL   He challenges Paul's assumption that the worst would inevitably happen: he would lose his job and be unable to find another one. He had no proof that this would be the case, and was wasting a lot of time and energy worrying about it.

CAN'T STAND IT   He challenges Paul's belief that he would not be able to cope if he lost his job. Although it would be difficult for him to cope, it would be in his own interest, and in the interest of his family, for him to do so.

SELF/OTHER RATING   Finally, Dr Bill challenges Paul's statement that he would be a failure if lost his job as a result of his back problems, and introduces him to the Raggy Doll Club. How could losing his job make him a weakling and of no value? He had to accept that he was a special person in himself, just like all the people he came in contact with – with faults and failings, strengths and weaknesses, all combining to make him who he is.

*

What all the above examples show us is that we often end up making impossible demands on ourselves and holding on to unhealthy beliefs. These lead to the negative emotional, physical and behavioural phenomena which produce toxic stress. Challenging these beliefs is the key to recovering.

Step Five

Challenging the Emotional and Behavioural Consequences of Stress

Most of us only recognise chronic stress and seek help for it once we experience the negative consequences arising from our unhealthy beliefs and demands. These consequences include emotional, physical and behavioural responses that need to be understood and, where appropriate, challenged.

The emotional consequences of chronic stress

The four most common emotional consequences of our unhealthy demands and beliefs are:

ANXIETY   Persistent feelings of worry and fear, giving rise to physical symptoms.

DEPRESSION   Persistent feelings of low mood, which often follow periods of prolonged anxiety. As with anxiety, these are often accompanied by physical symptoms.

LOW FRUSTRATION TOLERANCE (DISTURBANCE ANXIETY)
Annoyance or irritation that the world will not change to suit us. This too is usually associated with physical symptoms.

ANGER   Persistent feelings of extreme annoyance, at oneself or others.

Anxiety is associated with increased adrenalin, and depression with increased adrenalin and glucocorticol; the latter in particular leads to an increased risk of suicide. Low frustration tolerance and anger are more associated with noradrenalin, and carry significant risks to cardiac health.

We cannot block or change our emotional responses to stress, however uncomfortable they are. We must learn to accept the way we feel. It is more helpful to challenge the underlying unhealthy demands and beliefs, and our negative behavioural responses to them.

Let's examine a few simple examples of our emotional responses to chronic stress:

MICHAEL works in a company that is not doing well; he is unsure whether it is going to survive. This leads to a prolonged period of chronic stress. His demand is that he must be certain that he is not going to lose his job. This results in the emotion of anxiety.

JOHN, who has a history of depression, works in the same company. He too is incredibly stressed by the thought of losing his job, and eventually his mood begins to drop. His unhealthy belief that he is worthless leads to him slipping into depression.

NORA is another employee at the company and is also extremely stressed. She starts to experience the emotion of low frustration tolerance (disturbance anxiety) as she demands more information from management regarding the company's future.

MELISSA is another worker at risk of being let go from the same company. Her emotion is intense anger, aimed at the bosses of the company, arising from her view that 'they should not have got us into this mess to start with!'

It would be a waste of time to try and change or challenge these emotions. Imagine saying to Michael 'You must not be anxious' or to Melissa 'You must stop being angry'. We cannot simply turn emotions on or off.

The physical consequences of chronic stress

It is often the physical symptoms experienced as a result of our emotional responses to chronic stress that encourage us to seek help. This is because these symptoms can be so debilitating that they end up interfering with our daily lives. It is important to remember that our brain and body are connected, and that as a result emotions like anxiety and anger are usually associated with bodily sensations and symptoms. While most of these physical symptoms are usually not dangerous in themselves, they become a warning sign if they are present for long periods of time. In chronic stress, they are an indicator that we have high levels of noradrenalin and glucocortisol, with potentially lethal consequences. Many people reading this may not think they are suffering from toxic stress, but may identify with the physical symptoms that underlie it. Let's examine the main physical symptoms we may experience in response to particular emotions relevant to chronic stress.

ANXIETY:

- increased heart rate
- stomach in knots
- muscle tension
- headaches
- shortness of breath
- sweating
- feeling faint
- fatigue
- irritable bowel
- sleep difficulty
- lack of libido
- muscle pains

DEPRESSION:

- exhaustion
- sleep difficulties
- poor appetite
- lack of libido

LOW FRUSTRATION TOLERANCE AND ANGER:

- increased heart rate
- shallow breathing
- muscle tension
- fatigue
- lack of libido
- headaches

As with the emotional consequences of chronic stress, it is impossible try to stop all these physical symptoms, as they are the natural bodily responses to our emotions. It is extremely useful to identify them, however, as they are markers of the underlying hormonal barrages unleashed in toxic stress. What we *can* do is apply lifestyle changes and therapies to dampen down these physical responses.

The behavioural consequences of chronic stress

While we cannot challenge either the emotional or physical responses to stress, we can challenge our behavioural responses to it. In fact, how we behave in response to stress determines to a large extent how much at risk we are to the consequences of stress. Our behavioural responses to stress usually mirror the unhealthy demands and beliefs we are making!

We can divide behavioural responses to stress into four categories:

- Avoidant behaviour
- Safety behaviour
- Aggressive behaviour
- Toxic lifestyle behaviour

AVOIDANT BEHAVIOUR   This is common in those suffering from anxiety or depression due to chronic stress. In order to avoid the unpleasant physical responses, many try and avoid thinking about or dealing with the problem in question. In other cases, they avoid starting or finishing tasks due to fatigue. They may also avoid planning for the future. Examples of this are avoiding looking for a new job following redundancy, avoiding contacting the bank when a mortgage repayment is missed, or avoiding relationship counselling when one's relationship is in difficulties. This behaviour simply exacerbates the stress, and leads to further anxiety and low mood.

SAFETY BEHAVIOUR   This is also common in those suffering from anxiety or depression due to chronic stress. One way of coping with stress is to seek safety and security. A typical example would be where a person fears they are about to lose their job and constantly seeks reassurance from the company, or a person who is in financial difficulty spending more and more time going over bank statements.

AGGRESSIVE BEHAVIOUR This is common in those who respond to chronic stress with anger or low frustration tolerance. Aggression leads a person to express uncomfortable emotions in a physical manner. Examples of this would be road rage, explosive arguments over minor problems in the home, and an unwarranted outburst from an irate boss. Where alcohol is involved, these outbursts can become dangerously violent. Those who show aggressive behavioural patterns seem to be particularly susceptible to the health risks of toxic stress.

TOXIC LIFESTYLE BEHAVIOURS These are the most unrecognised consequences of toxic stress. While the physiological consequences of chronic stress are incredibly damaging to physical and mental health, the lifestyle behaviours can be just as problematic. When we experience many of the emotions and physical symptoms of stress, we often engage in the following behaviours:

- EATING UNHEALTHILY – we stop cooking properly and eating fresh fruit and vegetables. Instead, we eat processed food, missing key meals such as breakfast, and becoming deficient in key vitamins and nutrients;
- We often STOP EXERCISING on a daily basis and spend too much time watching TV;
- As a result, we may develop OBESITY, which brings with it a host of negative consequences, such as diabetes, heart disease, high blood pressure and back problems;
- DRINKING ALCOHOL to excess;
- USING ILLEGAL DRUGS such as cocaine or hash to cope, running the risk of serious consequences for physical and mental health;
- SMOKING MORE, increasing the risk of heart disease and lung cancer;
- Spending too much time on the INTERNET AND SOCIAL NETWORKING SITES, as well as gambling and gaming online.

While it would be a waste of time to challenge the physical symptoms or emotions underlying toxic stress, it is possible to challenge unhealthy behaviours. Here are some examples of Dr Bill changing such patterns of behaviour.

'I can't stop coughing!'

Jim goes to see Dr Bill with persistent coughing for the previous six months. He is a forty-four-year-old business executive who has spent the previous year in a state of constant stress due to difficulties in collecting money owed by clients. He is under pressure from his superiors to deliver results and has become highly anxious, leading to a range of unhealthy behaviours. He is staying late at work and becoming physically and mentally exhausted. He is eating junk food and drinking too much. As a result, he is sleeping poorly and has lost all interest in sex. He is also smoking up to forty cigarettes a day, and constantly drinking coffee. Following a medical examination, he is diagnosed with chronic bronchitis due to smoking. Jim's own father died from lung cancer; while Dr Bill reassures Jim that he does not suffer from this, his lifestyle requires dramatic changes if he is to avoid a similar fate. He challenges Jim's behaviour by making the following points:

- Jim is using cigarettes and coffee as a coping mechanism to deal with his stress. These habits are increasing his risk of cancer and heart disease;
- Jim's diet and lack of exercise are making him heavier and putting him at risk of diabetes and heart disease;
- His excessive alcohol intake could develop into a serious problem;
- His lifestyle is putting his job in jeopardy because of his increased risk of developing serious illness.

Jim implements Dr Bill's recommendations and six months later reports that he feels like a new man. He weighs a stone less, has stopped smoking, exercises for thirty minutes a day, and has a far healthier diet. He is spending less time working late and more time with his family. To his great surprise, he is performing better at work and is much less anxious about his future.

'I just can't believe that it was me that suffered a heart attack!'

Paul arrives in to see Dr Bill following a serious heart attack, after which he had to be resuscitated. At work, he is one of the firm's leading performers. He is just forty-two and is still shocked that he suffered a heart attack. He says he was 'too busy' for such an inconvenience! Paul fits into the type A personality category (competitive, aggressive, impulsive, impatient and goal-orientated). He had been under severe stress over the last five years while the company was being restructured. He is in charge of the redundancies, with fifty employees having been let go so far. He is renowned as being difficult to work with, with a tendency for making outbursts when he doesn't get his way. He separated from his partner two years previously, as she couldn't cope with his temper or his drinking binges. He is eating poorly and has put on several stone in weight. His main weekly exercise of playing football is more of an excuse for aggression rather than being done with the aim of getting fit. Despite this, and his heavy smoking, he is rarely sick; indeed, he views being sick as a form of weakness. He collapsed during a Monday-night football session, and only survived because a defibrillator was available nearby. Paul is quite fixed in relation to his thinking and behaviour, and tells Dr Bill that he is too busy to change his lifestyle. Dr Bill explains the links between stress, unhealthy behaviours, heart disease and premature death. Paul admits that he would prefer to stay alive, and asks for some advice. Dr Bill recommends that Paul do the following:

- stop smoking

- reduce his alcohol intake
- start working with a dietician to manage his weight
- take thirty minutes of brisk exercise every day
- temper his aggressive outbursts
- attend classes in mindfulness, and
- work with Dr Bill on the demands behind his aggressive behaviour.

Paul initially accepted Dr Bill's challenge but had regressed to his usual behaviour within three months, coming to the conclusion that Dr Bill was a 'quack' and didn't know what he was talking about. Paul died six months later from a massive heart attack. Not everybody wants to give up their unhealthy thinking patterns and lifestyle behaviours.

'I just couldn't go on!'

Maura is referred to Dr Bill by her own doctor following a suicide attempt. She is accompanied by her partner, having spent more than a week on a life-support machine. She has found herself in a financial nightmare: she and her partner have both lost their jobs and are being hounded by the banks because of debts and mortgage arrears. The stress of this persisted for more than a year, and resulted in constant rows between her and her partner. She smoked constantly and stopped eating, with her family and friends becoming worried about her weight loss. Her anxiety eventually led to low mood, and she had become increasingly withdrawn and apathetic. Eventually, her partner was unable to cope with what he perceived as her apparent rejection of him, and her general behaviour, and had moved out to stay with his family.

Maura became increasingly consumed by toxic stress, her mood hit rock bottom, and she felt she couldn't go on. She thought the world would be a better place without her and even checked her life assurance to see how much her partner would get in the event of her death. She went from shop to shop and built up a potentially lethal supply of paracetamol. She took out the bottle of wine and consumed all the tablets, eventually becoming comatose. Fortunately, her sister, who had been worried about her, called round. When Maura finally regained consciousness ten days later, she was filled with a mixture of emotions: guilt at what she had done, and sadness that she had not been successful. Her partner is now back by her side – upset with himself that he had not recognised how depressed she was. She accepts Dr Bill's help in trying to sort out her emotional problems. Dr Bill is extremely supportive and helpful and is able to show both Maura and her partner how the prolonged period of stress had triggered her depression and how this had led to suicidal thoughts and actions.

He offers to help her deal with her depression but points out that this will involve making significant changes to her life relating to diet, supplements, exercise, and counselling and drug therapy. He goes on to challenge many of the toxic lifestyle behaviours she had developed as a result of her stress, explaining to her how they were continuing to contribute to her difficulties. They agree that Maura will make the following changes:

- stop smoking
- stop drinking alcohol until her mood has returned to normal

- eat a healthier diet and take supplements
- exercise for at least thirty minutes every day
- seek financial advice
- work out a new arrangement with the bank, and
- attend counselling with her partner.

Both Maura and her partner agree to the above and are committed to making the necessary changes. The bank is very accommodating when they learn of her situation. Nine months on, she is back at work in a new job. She feels much better: she is not drinking alcohol or smoking, is exercising daily and is taking regular supplements. She spends some time working with Dr Bill on her negative thoughts using simple CBM/CBT concepts. She has also accepted his offer of developing mindfulness and spends fifteen minutes a day learning to be 'in the present'. A year later, she is pregnant, and the house, which was previously so full of sorrow, becomes full of joy.

There are many lessons to be learned from this story:

- Toxic stress builds up if we do not act in time. For example, Maura should have sought financial assistance much earlier;
- Chronic stress can lead to a major bout of depression;
- Stress is often worsened by poor diet, lack of exercise and increased alcohol consumption;
- Suicidal thoughts and actions are a potentially lethal but avoidable consequence of toxic stress. Acting on these thoughts can sentence those left behind to a lifetime of grief;

- The earlier you come for help, the easier it will be to get on the road back to health. If you have become extremely distressed, open up to someone close to you. This step is usually the hardest to take;

- If you ever find yourself in this situation, take that first step! It may end up saving your life and preventing the destruction of the lives of those you love.

Step Six

Putting It All Together:

A Working Model of Toxic Stress

The last few chapters have demonstrated how to identify chronic stress in our lives. They have also covered how to evaluate and challenge:

- stressors and our interpretation of them (CHALLENGING THE 'A')
- our unhealthy beliefs and the demands we place on ourselves (CHALLENGING THE 'B'), and
- the emotional, physical and behavioural consequences of such beliefs and demands (CHALLENGING THE 'C').

To challenge the 'A', 'B' and 'C', we must put our responses to stress into a structured model to enable us to make sense of our situation. Below are a number of examples which show this process in action, and how Dr Bill uses this model to help various people reduce their risk of developing the serious physical and psychological consequences of toxic stress.

'It brought it all back!'

Jane is brought to see Dr Bill by her sister Maura. She had been in a state of chronic stress for over eight months but managed to keep it all hidden until finally cracking under the strain and succumbing to a bout of depression. She had taken an overdose but, luckily, had survived when she was discovered in time by Maura, who was bringing her new baby around to meet her.

Maura knew that Jane was keeping something from her but was unable to get her to reveal what was bothering her. In fact, Jane's difficulties started to arise when Maura had approached her during her pregnancy to ask her to act as godmother to her future child if all went well.

What Maura didn't know was that Jane had five years earlier found herself pregnant just as her then boyfriend walked out on her. It was a nightmare time for her as she was both financially and emotionally vulnerable. She had attended a clinic in Dublin, where it was suggested that a 'termination' would be the best way forward, and that they could arrange for her to travel to London to have it performed. Her mind was a blur – filled with emotions of hurt and loss due to her relationship breakdown, and ashamed that her mum and dad, who are extremely conservative, would react badly to her situation. She also felt that her future career prospects would be seriously affected if the pregnancy continued.

She eventually had the termination, and on her return managed to block out what had occurred, and pick up the pieces of her life. However, her sister's innocent request triggers her emotional brain into action, and her stress levels rise further as Maura's pregnancy gets closer to term. She becomes fatigued, has difficulty sleeping, loses interest in food, and loses interest in sex with her partner, who feels rejected. Finally, her mood plummets and suicide thoughts arrive: 'I don't deserve to keep on living, and my secret can die with me.' The full weight of toxic stress arrived, putting her life at risk.

Dr Bill teases out the facts of the situation. Her mood is still extremely down; he explains that they will have to target that. He lays out a holistic approach involving exercise, nutrition, supplements and avoiding alcohol, and finally suggests a course of antidepressants – all of which she agrees to. He sees her regularly until he is happy that her mood is back to normal. As promised, he then offers to help her deal with her original stressor. They move on to do an 'ABC' of the problem.

A. *Trigger*: Her termination.
Inference/Danger:
- That as a result of terminating her pregnancy, she had in effect killed her own child;
- That she felt very sad that she would never see the child;
- That she would struggle to cope if those close to her became aware of her actions;
- That she was upset that she had allowed herself to be convinced by the clinic to agree to the termination and could not forgive herself for making that decision;
- That she felt she was a failure as a result of her actions.

B. *Belief/Demands*:
- She should have made a different decision and not terminated her pregnancy;
- She was afraid that others would become aware of her secret;

- She believed she was a complete failure as a person as a result of her decision.

C. *Consequences*:

Emotions: Guilt, shame and depression.

Physical reactions: Fatigue, poor concentration, muscle tension, stomach upset, difficulty sleeping, and weight loss due to lack of interest in food.

Behaviour – Jane:

- tries to hide her secret from those close to her
- ruminates constantly on what she perceives as a disastrous period of her life
- stops eating and loses interest in sex, and
- tries to avoid thinking about the arrival of her sister's new baby, as it makes her feel worse.

Dr Bill proceeds to assist her in challenging these issues.

CHALLENGING THE 'A' They agree that there is little point in trying to deny that the termination had led to the death of her baby or that she had denied herself the possibility of seeing the child grow up. These were realities. However, she could challenge whether her emotional visualisation of how those close to her would treat her if her 'secret' came out was valid. Had she any proof that it would be as awful as she visualised? They agree that it would be better to examine her underlying beliefs and demands.

CHALLENGING THE 'B' Dr Bill helps her to see that her absolute demand that she should not have made the decision to go for termination was at the heart of all her difficulties. This unhealthy demand, and her rating of herself and perceived rating by others if they learned of what she had done, were the underlying basis for her guilt, shame and depression.

Dr Bill persuades Jane that the best way to become well again is to learn how to challenge these unhealthy beliefs/demands. He explains the concepts behind the 'Big MACS', and together they come up with the following:

MUST He explains the concept of absolute demands like 'must', 'should', 'should not', and so on. They agree that her absolute demand that she should be able to 'rewrite' her decision about going for the termination was unhealthy. Most of us in life, he explained, make decisions that at a later stage we wish we could alter. It is the nature of being human to do so. In practice, we have to go back to the circumstances surrounding the decision. She was in a very vulnerable state emotionally due to the breakdown of her relationship and the feelings of isolation and being on her own in relation to bringing up a future child. She had to accept that although it might be preferable if she had made a different decision, the circumstances at the time created an obstacle to this. Once she accepted that we can only make a particular decision based on the factors in play at the time, she would find it easier to accept what had happened – even if she had justifiable regrets about these things.

SELF/OTHER RATING Dr Bill then moves on to help her challenge her rating of herself, and indeed her accepting of other people's rating if they discovered her secret. They spend a lot of time examining the importance of the Raggy Doll Club; she finds this concept incredibly powerful. She and others could rate her behaviour in terms of going for a termination but could not rate her as a person – as she was just a Raggy Doll!

CHALLENGING THE 'C' They decide that Jane must accept her emotional reactions as normal and do nothing to change them. Her physical symptoms were also normal responses to her emotions. But they decide that challenging her unhealthy behaviours would be of assistance. They decide:

- It was better to cease her constant negative reflections on what had happened and decide instead to write down her thougts in an 'ABC' manner if these thoughts persist;
- It was better to embrace the arrival of her new godchild in a positive manner, as avoiding doing so would only worsen her problems;
- That she had to continue the positive lifestyle changes already suggested in relation to exercise, and so on;
- That she had to cease trying to hide her secret and in fact might be advised to tell her sister about her past.

'We do nothing but fight!'

Jean comes to see Dr Bill complaining of a host of symptoms: exhaustion, lack of sex drive, and impaired short-term memory and concentration. She has two children and works part-time in a call centre; she is struggling to make ends meet. Her partner Kevin finds it difficult to hold down a job, which is a cause of tension in the house. Fortunately, they are renting and do not have the added pressure of a mortgage. Nonetheless, Jean finds juggling her work with ferrying the kids to school difficult. If Kevin was not working, he had time to help, but could not contribute to the household financially, and vice versa. As a result, she becomes very anxious and upset, and after a period where Kevin is out of work for a long time, they argue constantly, and she stops eating properly. Jean's mother observes her rapid weight loss and is convinced that she is physically ill. Following some tests carried out by Dr Bill, it becomes clear that the problem is chronic stress. She tells Dr Bill about the tense atmosphere in the house and that she and her partner (whom she still loves) did 'nothing but fight'.

Dr Bill advises Jean on her lifestyle, nutrition, exercise and alcohol consumption. Her most pressing problem is financial, due to her partner losing his job. They decide to do an 'ABC' of the problem.

A. *Trigger*: Her partner loses his part-time job.
    Inference/Danger:
- They will once again be short of money;
- They will find it increasingly difficult to pay the bills;
- They will be unable to pay the rent and eventually be evicted.

B. *Belief/Demands*:
- They must be able to pay their bills;
- If they cannot, she will be unable to cope;
- She will have failed her children.

C. *Consequences*:
    Emotions: Anxiety, frustration and depression.
    Physical reactions: Fatigue, headaches, muscle tension, stomach upset, teeth grinding at night and weight loss due to loss of interest in food.
    Behaviour – Jean:
- ruminates constantly on her fears that they will be unable to pay their bills and will be evicted
- refuses to open any post in case it is from the bank or credit card company

- stops eating and can't sleep at night
- rings her mother constantly, looking for assurance, and
- takes out her frustration on her partner by constantly fighting with him.

Dr Bill proceeds to assist her in challenging these behaviours.

CHALLENGING THE 'A' They decide that there is little benefit in challenging her inferences and the perceived danger, as they were a realistic assessment of the situation.

CHALLENGING THE 'B' Dr Bill helps her challenge her demand that they must be able to pay their pay bills and that if they could not, she would be a failure and would be unable to cope. Dr Bill persuades Jean that the best way out of her problem is to learn how to challenge these unhealthy demands.

He explains the concepts behind the 'Big MACS', and together they come up with the following:

MUST Dr Bill challenges her demand that she and her partner must be able to pay their bills. He points out that she does not have complete control over this. It would be preferable if Kevin could find work, but this may not be possible; her demand for complete certainty was unhealthy.

AWFUL He challenges Jean's assumption that the worst would inevitably happen. She does not have any proof that her emotional visualisation of what was going to take place was true.

Was it not equally possible that both she and her partner might end up working again and that their financial situation might become secured once more?

CAN'T STAND IT   He challenges Jean's belief that she would not be able to cope if everything she feared came true. It would certainly be extremely difficult if her family was evicted, but she would cope.

SELF/OTHER RATING   Finally, he challenges her statement that she would be a failure and introduces her to the Raggy Doll Club. The day she became a Raggy Doll, she would cease rating herself, regardless of whether her financial problems were resolved.

CHALLENGING THE 'C'   They decide that Jean must accept her emotional reactions as normal and do nothing to change them. Her physical symptoms were also normal responses to her emotions. Dr Bill recommends exercise, yoga and mindfulness as ways in which she could deal with her emotional responses.

He challenges her behavioural responses:

- Continuous negative thinking about the consequences of falling into debt was not helping her deal with the problem;
- Working out a solution with her credit-card company or contacting MABS would be a more useful response;
- Smoking and drinking were not helping her deal with the issues;

- Better nutrition, taking supplements and getting exercise would be a better way to cope;
- Fighting with her partner was only making the situation worse;
- Seeking constant reassurance from others was not getting her anywhere.

Jean begins to implement some of these recommendations in her life. Her chronic stress, anxiety and physical symptoms start to disappear. She still struggles with money but has learned how to deal with financial issues in a positive manner.

'Who am I?'

Jim is referred to Dr Bill when his parents, to their horror, find him at home attaching a rope to the attic. He is eighteen years old and in Leaving Cert class at school. He has been in real trouble physically and mentally for the previous two years and was suffering from all the classical signs of toxic stress. He had lost weight, was quite down, was getting continuous mouth ulcers and was having difficulties with sleep, food and concentration. He was also feeling exhausted for large parts of the day.

His parents had assumed that all of these things were due to the typical stress experienced when heading into state exams. Jim's issues were, however, deeper and more sinister. He had always been quite shy and bookish. He had a few interactions with girls, but felt awkward and uncomfortable in their presence.

Unfortunately, this had led to a two-year period of being unmercifully mocked and bullied by a hard-core element in the school. Word was put out that he was gay, and this had a profoundly upsetting effect on Jim, who began to question his sexuality and indeed his self-esteem. He experienced continuous 'techno bullying' in the form of nasty text messages and Facebook comments, and on one occasions found himself being filmed on a mobile phone after being 'roughed up'. He was afraid of broaching the issue at home or at school due to his fear of inviting more bullying.

He began to feel trapped, and his stress levels rose. He was already coping with the pressure of upcoming exams; it was all too much. Suicide thoughts were coming more and more. It would be for the best. Maybe then there would be some peace – for he had reached a stage where he no longer knew who he was.

His mood dropped further, and he saw no other way out. Luckily, his mother came back to the house earlier than expected, and disaster was averted.

Dr Bill spends some time with Jim and puts together all the pieces. It was clear that the lad was suffering from chronic stress and low mood. He arranges to have him assessed by the psychiatric team. The school moves in, with the help of parents, to tackle the bullies. In the meantime, they decide that it would be helpful to examine both his lifestyle and the issues that had led to the problem.

He suggests a holistic approach of proper nutrition, daily exercise, supplements, avoiding alcohol, some counselling and, if it was felt necessary by the specialist, possibly a course of anti-depressants.

In fact, the latter is not required: Jim's mood improves by itself due to the relief of opening up about his problems, the improvement in the situation at school, and the changes in relation to nutrition, supplements, counselling and exercise. But he is still struggling with his original identity issues. He asks Dr Bill for some help.

Together they examine the problem, and come up with the following 'ABC':

A. *Trigger*: Being bullied, as his schoolmates assume he is gay.

Inference/Danger:

- That because they think he is gay, this must make it true;
- He finds himself attracted to girls but very shy about relationships;
- That this was leading to him being very confused about his sexual identity;
- He felt, as a result, that he was of no value;
- That he could understand them picking on him: 'Wasn't he worthless anyway?'

B. *Belief/Demands*:

- Because of his confusion over his sexuality, he was a complete failure and of no worth;
- That others will find out about his confusion and judge him appropriately.

C. *Consequences*:

Emotions: Depression, shame.

Physical reactions: Fatigue, weight loss due to lack of interest in food, difficulty with concentration.

Behaviour – Jim:

- tries to avoid contact with girls due to his confusion
- withdraws from contact with many of his classmates, as he is afraid they will broach the subject or mock him
- stops eating, sleeping and taking exercise

- spends a lot of time on the internet trying to find answers to his confusion – but none come
- avoids sharing his difficulties with his parents, as he is worried that they will be upset, and
- is falling behind in his studies, as his emotional brain is full to the brim with negative thoughts.

Dr Bill proceeds to assist him in challenging these behaviours.

CHALLENGING THE 'A' They decide that it is helpful to challenge his assertion that just because he is shy in his dealings with girls, he is gay. Is he not mixing up being anxious in social situations with his sexual identity?

They also agree that just because his classmates thought he was gay did not mean that he actually was. Could they look into his world? Would they not be quite surprised that his favourite actress was Angeline Jolie, who he thought was 'hot stuff'? That there was no evidence to back up either their, or indeed his own, fear that he was gay. In fact, everything pointed to the opposite!

CHALLENGING THE 'B' Dr Bill moves on and examines Jim's belief that he is worthless. He introduces him to the Raggy Doll Club, and Jim begins to realise that he is not allowed to rate himself or accept the rating of his schoolmates under any circumstances. He at last feels free – and has a good laugh at the Raggy Doll Club when he finds the original cartoon series on the internet.

CHALLENGING THE 'C' They move on to examine Jim's unhealthy

behaviour patterns, which were worsening the situation. They decide that he will:

- exercise and eat properly
- avoid alcohol for the time being
- plan, when his exams were over, to put himself in the way of meeting girls (Dr Bill would give him some tips about social anxiety)
- open up a dialogue with his parents
- avoid negative sites on the web, which could lead him down dark roads
- stay in regular contact with his school counsellor, and
- report any recurrences of bullying to teachers and his parents.

A year later, Jim has got his exams and is in first year in college. He is dating a cool blonde, who falls for his gentleness and sense of humour. His former classmates are now envious! Most of all, he has become a real Raggy Doll: he helps on the college website and helplines to reach other people in trouble. Jim has learned a vital message: that no matter how stressed we get, or how confused we may be about life issues, the secret is to open up and talk!

'I feel so useless!'

After working for thirty years in a local factory, Tony ends up taking an early-retirement redundancy package at the age of sixty-three. His three children have all long since left home and are now living their own lives in different parts of the country. His wife Mary had been looking forward to Tony's retirement for a number of years but, as often happens in life, things had not work out as planned.

Tony had been used to a life which was highly structured and organised. His social life had centred on his workplace and interaction with workmates; he finds retirement to be a very isolating and lonely experience.

He starts to become increasingly stressed. Mary notices that he seems fatigued and is not sleeping well. He often mopes around the house and becomes irritable and difficult to live with. He begins to drink more at home and stops frequenting old haunts where his workmates would congregrate. He also starts to develop headaches. Finally, she gets him to check his blood pressure at the local pharmacy. It is noted to be high. She finally persuades him to attend Dr Bill, who quickly gets to the core of the problem.

Having dealt with Tony's high blood pressure and reviewed his lifestyle (with a special emphasis on exercise and reducing his levels of alcohol intake), Dr Bill moves on to help Tony examine his stress issues. They put together the following 'ABC':

A.   *Trigger*: His retirement.
Inference/Danger:
- He feels that since he retired, he no longer has any value to either his wife or those around him;
- Due to the fact that his work environment had been his main source of socialising, he feels quite isolated and alone;
- He feels embarrassed to meet up with former colleagues, as they are still doing an important job, while he is now only an outside observer.

B.   *Belief/Demands*: Because he is no longer working, he is of no value as a person.

C.   *Consequences*:
       Emotions – Tony:
- ruminates constantly about the hopelessness and uselessness of his life since retirement
- avoids socialising in the local haunts of his former workmates
- becomes irritable and difficult to live with
- eats poorly and stops taking exercise
- drinks excessively at home
- avoids becoming involved in any other social or sporting activities in the community, and
- spends too much time moping around the house.

CHALLENGING THE 'A' They decide that they could challenge Tony's inference that he is of no value since his retirement. Could he prove that this was indeed so? Did he have any proof that his emotional visualisation, that his workmates would not want to meet him simply because he was retired, was accurate? Confronting these statements would help, but it was really his deep-seated beliefs about himself that he needed to examine.

CHALLENGING THE 'B' Dr Bill encourages Tony to challenge this unhealthy belief. He explains the concepts behind the 'Big MACS', and together they decide that his main problem lies in his rating of himself.

SELF/OTHER RATING He challenges Tony's statement that he is a failure because he is no longer working. He introduces him to the Raggy Doll Club – and the idea that he is special as a person. As a Raggy Doll, although he was not allowed to rate himself as a person or accept the rating of his work colleagues, he could take a look at his behaviour to see if there were areas of his life since retirement that he could change.

CHALLENGING THE 'C' They decide that Tony has to accept his emotional responses to this stressor – depression – as normal. His physical symptoms are also a natural response to the way he is feeling. But Dr Bill challenges Tony's behavioural responses as follows:

- Constant rumination about his situation was not helpful: it would be better to write down the main issues, as outlined above, and challenge them;
- He would have to find a new 'passion' in his life. This might involve engaging in a wide new range of interests, to find some that appealed to him;
- He should look on this as an exciting new chapter in his life, opening up a new world of opportunities;
- In particular, he should examine the possibility of taking up some valuable voluntary work in the community, as this would have a very positive impact on his image of himself;
- He had to examine key areas like exercise, nutrition and alcohol intake in order to remain physically and mentally well during his retirement years;
- He should reconnect with his former workmates and share with them his new passions: it would be them who would finally be the envious ones!

'My life is a living hell!'

Mark is sent to Dr Bill after a serious suicide attempt. He had taken a drug overdose and ended up spending a week in intensive care. He is a middle manager in a large company; he is being bullied by a new, abrasive boss who has been sent in to 'cut corners' and increase profit margins. Mark is married with two young children and is a conscientious, hard-working employee; he is usually first in and last out of the office. But for the year prior to his suicide attempt, his life was a living hell: he had begun to suffer from toxic stress. His boss mocked him in front of other staff and was impossible to please. Mark was feeling exhausted, had trouble sleeping, and could no longer concentrate properly. He developed cold sores and mouth ulcers, and lost interest in food. He started drinking more and became irritable. His mood and self-esteem began to drop. He became more withdrawn at home and spent hours late at night staring aimlessly at a computer screen or watching TV. Things came to a head when his boss began to drop hints that several jobs, including his, would have to be shed. Finally, he began to believe that there was no way out of his situation and that he was of no worth; he started to plan his suicide. Although he loved his wife and children dearly, he thought they would be better off without him around. He wrote a note for his wife explaining his decision the day before the suicide attempt. He then took an overdose.

Fortunately, his wife arrived home early, found him unconscious and got help. Following his discharge from hospital, she brought him to see Dr Bill. Mark is in two minds about the fact that he survived the suicide attempt. When he sees how much his wife cares about him, he is relieved that he was not successful. Nonetheless, his problems at work remain. Is still being alive only prolonging the agony?

Dr Bill empathises with him and is pleased that he has already been seen by a psychiatrist and prescribed an anti-depressant. He gives Mark lifestyle advice, suggesting that he take more exercise, eat properly, cease drinking alcohol and take time off work. They agree that it would be beneficial to send a report to his personnel department detailing the problems he has experienced.

Dr Bill explains how chronic stress can lead to a range of physical and emotional problems; in Mark's case, it led to depression and suicidal thoughts. If Mark is to get better, he will have to change his thinking and behaviour. Mark returns in a few weeks: by that time, his mood has improved and he is better able to concentrate. Dr Bill explains the concept of the 'ABC' approach, and together they work out the following analysis of his problem:

A.   *Trigger*: Being bullied by his boss.
      Inference/Danger:
- He doesn't think he will ever be able to please his boss;
- He feels trapped in his job;

B.   *Belief/Demands*:
- He feels like a failure;
- He can't cope with work anymore;
- His boss must not treat him in this way.

C.   *Consequences*:
      Emotions: Hurt, anxiety and depression.
      Physical reactions: Fatigue, muscle tension, bowel spasms, weight loss.
      Behaviour – **Mark**:
- ruminates constantly about the way his boss is treating him

- worries about how stressful work will be when he returns
- avoids phone calls from work, and
- refuses to talk things through with his wife.

Dr Bill then helps Mark challenge these things.

CHALLENGING THE 'A' They decide that while they could challenge the interpretation that his boss would never treat him fairly or that he would remain trapped in this situation, it might be difficult to guarantee that these realities could be changed. It would be simpler and more effective to challenge his underlying unhealthy beliefs and demands.

CHALLENGING THE 'B' Dr Bill persuades him that the most effective way to deal with his problems is to learn how to challenge his unhealthy demands. He explains the concepts behind the 'Big MACS', and together they come up with the following:

MUST Dr Bill challenges Mark's demand that his boss must change his treatment of him. He has to accept that he cannot control his boss's behaviour and that his belief that he will not be able to return to work unless things change fundamentally is unhealthy.

AWFUL Dr Bill challenges Mark's assumption that the worst will inevitably happen. Mark has no proof that he will lose his job.

CAN'T STAND IT Dr Bill challenges Mark's belief that he would not be able to cope if he lost his job, or if his boss continued to bully him. In fact, he could learn to deal with both situations, if it was in his own or his family's interests to do so.

SELF/OTHER RATING Finally, Dr Bill challenges Mark's statement that he is a failure and introduces him to the Raggy Doll Club. How could his boss treating him negatively make Mark a failure! If he accepts that he is a Raggy Doll, he can learn to challenge this misconception.

CHALLENGING THE 'C' They decide that Mark has to accept his emotional responses of hurt, anxiety and depression as normal. His physical symptoms are also a natural response to the way he is feeling. But Dr Bill challenges Mark's behavioural responses in a number of areas:

- Avoiding the company by not answering calls from them was not helping him deal with his issues;
- Discussing matters with the personnel department and other superiors would be more productive;
- Requesting a transfer was a possible option, rather than worrying about returning to the same situation;
- Not eating properly and drinking alcohol was not improving his situation;
- Improving his diet, taking supplements and exercising would be more helpful;
- Not discussing matters with his wife was holding back his recovery;
- Counselling could also be of benefit to help him deal with his situation.

Mark starts to understand what triggered his depression and works with Dr Bill to improve his situation. He releases the burden of worry he has been carrying around and becomes less anxious and depressed. He tries to resolve the situation with the company and is transferred to a new section. When his boss finds out the effects his behaviour has had on Mark, he is deeply sorry and tries to help Mark get back to work. Mark's relationship has recovered, and he has started doing charity work to help others who are in a similar situation to the one he was in. He has started exercising, eating properly, meditating and putting his personal life before work. Mark's case shows just how dangerous toxic stress can be to a person's mental health.

'I feel invisible!'

Seamus is referred to Dr Bill by his wife, who has become increasingly concerned about his lack of energy and difficulty sleeping. They are the classical modern couple. Both were extremely successful in their careers and only married in their mid-thirties. After two years, they decided to try for their first child, and the difficulties began.

His wife Joan struggled to conceive and became obsessed with becoming pregnant. After all, her friends had all become pregnant very easily; she couldn't understand that she would be the one who would struggle! She was used to 'controlling' all aspects of her life and tried to apply the same principles to fertility.

Following intensive attempts at conceiving (where at times Seamus felt as if he had been reduced to a 'sperm machine'), and subsequent fruitless investigations, Joan became increasingly anxious and stressed. Finally, they are referred for IVF treatment for infertility, and on the third attempt Joan becomes pregnant.

She delivers a beautiful little girl, and the 'bundle' arrives into their lives. After the two years of hell trying to conceive, Joan is determined that nothing will go wrong with their precious infant and devotes all her energies to caring for her.

Seamus quickly learns to take a 'back seat' and allow the maternal bonds to develop. Joan becomes so infatuated with her new daughter that, without realising it, she 'sidelines' her husband. It is only when, nine months later, he complains of exhaustion and of struggling to eat and sleep that she notices that he is not himself and suggestst that he go to see Dr Bill.

Seamus struggles to open up to the doctor. 'I don't know how to explain how I feel,' he blurts out. 'All I know is that I feel like crap!'

Dr Bill helps him to verbalise how he feels. He ascertains that Seamus has been quite down for the previous three months, with fatigue, poor concentration, and loss of interest in food, sex and general activities. He has become quite apathethic about his work and has even struggled to relate to his new daughter, whom he 'adored'.

Seamus, with Dr Bill's assistance, begins to describe his feelings of 'being invisible' since the odyssey into the world of IVF and parenthood started. He loved Joan but felt 'shut out', and of no relevance. When they examined his behavioural response to how he felt, it became clear that he was drinking too much, had stopped exercising, was eating poorly, and was spending too much time online.

Dr Bill felt that Seamus was a typical example of 'postnatal male depression', following a prolonged period of toxic stress which had begun with the IVF process. He explained that many men who had been through such experiences often felt the same; this helped him realise that his situation was not particularly unusual.

Dr Bill does some blood tests. The tests come back normal, and they decide on an intensive lifestyle programme to see if he could improve the way he felt without the use of drug therapy. Following this, Seamus agrees to return to examine his issues, using the 'ABC' process outlined by Dr Bill.

One month later, Seamus comes back to see Dr Bill. He is starting to feel better due to his relief at opening up to how he had been feeling and the results of doing intensive exercise, taking supplements, avoiding alcohol, and reducing his internet usage. Together, they come up with the following analysis of his problem:

A. *Trigger*: The arrival of his new daughter.
   Inference/Danger:
   - That, although he loves the new arrival, he feels excluded from the special mother–baby relationship that ensued;
   - That because he was a man, it was inappropriate for him to say how he felt, as he would be mocked for 'not coping properly';
   - That he felt invisible to his wife and all those who came to visit to enthuse about the new arrival;
   - That Joan no longer found him interesting or of importance in her life as a result of the new arrival;
   - This in turn led him to feel of no value in himself.
B. *Belief/Demands*: He felt a failure.
C. *Consequences*:
   Emotions: Depression.
   Physical reactions: Fatigue, poor concentration, and muscle tightness.

Behaviour – Seamus:
- begins to drink excessively
- eats poorly and goes to bed late, as he struggles to sleep
- ruminates constantly on the unfairness of having to try to compete with his beautiful new daughter for the attention of Joan, and
- spends too much time on the internet.

Dr Bill helps Hugh challenge these thoughts and behaviours.

CHALLENGING THE 'A' They decide that Seamus could challenge his emotional visualisation that he was invisible to his wife Joan and those close to them. Could he prove that just because Joan was spending a lot of time with their new child, he no longer mattered to her? They could also challenge his assumption that he should hide how he felt, simply because he was a man. Was it helpful for him to conceal his feelings?

CHALLENGING THE 'B' Dr Bill persuades Seamus that although challenging his 'A' was extremely helpful, the best approach would be to challenge the unhealthy demands he was making. He explains the concepts behind the 'Big MACS', and together they decide that his primary problem relates to his rating of himself.

SELF/OTHER RATING He challenges Seamus's statement that he is a failure because he perceives that he is of no value to Joan, or indeed to those around him, and introduces him to the Raggy Doll Club.

CHALLENGING THE 'C' They decide that Seamus could not challenge his natural reactions of depression, or his physical symptoms, but that he could challenge his behavioural responses in the following ways:

- Was drinking excessively, eating poorly and spending long periods online helping him feel better about himself?

- Would exercise, proper nutrition, ceasing alcohol and going to bed earlier not be a better option?

- Was constantly ruminating about how useless he was helping him deal with the situation?

- Would discussing with Joan how he felt, and looking for her assistance in dealing with his difficulties, not be more useful?

- Would seeking out hotels with a 'baby-friendly' environment not be a way of spending more 'romantic' times together and nourishing their relationship?

Six months later, Seamus and Joan are in a new space. Joan has developed more insight into the place of her new daughter in their lives. The infant is now a part of the collective household, rather than the only thing in their lives! Seamus has corrected many of his toxic-stress behaviours. Romance is definitely back on the horizon, and both of them look forward to the little breaks that Seamus now insists they take. Most of all, he is no longer invisible. The Raggy Doll Club has entered their lives!

'I can't let them down!'

Hugh is the founder of a small company which employs a staff of six, who work well together. During the economic boom, the company had done very well, and the staff shared in the profits. However, after a two-year battle with toxic stress, Hugh visits Dr Bill in a terrible state: he is constantly tired, is not sleeping or eating well, feels extremely anxious, has tension headaches and panic attacks, finds it difficult to concentrate, and suffers from low mood. These symptoms started when the recession began, and orders stopped coming into the company. Exchange-rate difficulties had reduced profits, and the banks had not been very helpful. The company was struggling to survive.

By the time Hugh comes to Dr Bill, he is convinced that that he must have a serious illness: Hugh's father died from heart disease in his late fifties, and Hugh is approaching that age. He is married with three children in their teens; his wife finally convinces him to go for help when he starts to get chest pains. He has started smoking again (after having given up), and is drinking more than twice the recommended amount. He has lost weight and cannot motivate himself to exercise.

Dr Bill investigates Hugh thoroughly, and rules out any possible illnesses. His symptoms are the warning signs of toxic stress. Dr Bill explains the risks of toxic stress, especially considering his family history. They decide to tackle the problem together. First, they deal with Hugh's lifestyle. Dr Bill gives Hugh advice on diet, exercise and nutrition, and strongly challenges his smoking and alcohol consumption.

Hugh accepts his advice and begins to change his whole lifestyle. But his problems at work remain, and he asks Dr Bill for advice on how to deal with this source of stress. They agree that if he is going to get better, he has to change his thinking and behaviour. Dr Bill explains the 'ABC' approach, and together they work out the following analysis of his problem:

A. *Trigger*: Hugh's company getting into financial difficulties.

Inference/Danger:

- He would have to let employees go to avoid the company going into administration;
- He would find it very difficult to fire staff to whom he had become close;
- The banks were making the company's situation worse;
- He must not have to sack his employees;
- He would have a very poor opinion of himself if he had to;
- If he does, he will feel he has failed them.

C. *Consequences*:

Emotions: Severe anxiety

Physical reactions: Fatigue, headaches, muscle tension, weight loss, chest pains

Behaviour – Hugh:

- ruminates constantly about having to let staff go
- stops eating properly
- sleeps poorly
- constantly reduces his company's costs in an attempt to avoid having to make redundancies
- avoids contact with the banks, and
- drinks and smokes too much.

Dr Bill helps Hugh challenge these thoughts and behaviours.

CHALLENGING THE 'A' They could challenge his inference that the company might reach a point where he would be forced by the bank to fire employees or let it go into administration, but at the moment this looked like a real possibility.

CHALLENGING THE 'B' Dr Bill persuades Hugh that the best approach would be to challenge the unhealthy demands he was making. He explains the concepts behind the 'Big MACS', and together they come up with the following:

MUST First, he challenges Hugh's demand that he must not let any of his employees go. While Hugh obviously doesn't want to do this, he might have to do so.

AWFUL He challenges Hugh's assumption that the worst would inevitably happen. He did not know how things would turn out; he was becoming stressed about a hypothetical scenario. If he did have to let employees go, it might not be as bad as he feared. He should also consider the possibility that he might be able to rehire them if the economy started to recover.

CAN'T STAND IT He challenges Hugh's belief that he would not be able to cope if he had to let employees go. It would be in the interest of the company and the remaining employees to do so.

SELF/OTHER RATING Finally, he challenges Hugh's statement that having to lay employees off would mean he is a failure, and introduces him to the Raggy Doll Club.

CHALLENGING THE 'C' They decide that Hugh could not challenge his natural reactions of anxiety, or his physical symptoms, but that he could challenge his behavioural responses, in the following ways:

- Avoiding communicating with the banks was not helping;
- Discussing financial matters with advisors and accountants may be a more productive use of his time and energy;
- Smoking and drinking more was just making matters worse;
- Improving his diet, taking supplements and doing exercise would be more helpful;
- Ruminating over his difficulties was only increasing his stress.

'There is no future for me!'

Sean is twenty-four and finds himself in a rut. He was enticed to leave school before completing his Leaving Cert by the high wages being offered on the building sites. It was a great life: with his pocket full of cash, he went out with his friends every night. Once the construction industry collapsed, however, so did his world. His skills were no longer required and he could not find work; his lack of education or other skills meant that he found it impossible to secure other employment. He went back to live at home and became withdrawn and stressed. He drank to cope with his stress, his self-esteem plummeted, and he gave up applying for jobs. He started arguing with his girlfriend, and his relationship broke down. His only consolation was that most of his friends were in a similar situation. He lost weight and developed cold sores and acne, and started getting tension headaches. His mood dropped and he started to think about ending his life: like many young men under the age of twenty-five, his prospects seemed bleak.

He went out drinking with friends, who tried to lift him out of his withdrawn mood – but to no avail. Sean left the pub and headed for the river. On his way, a poster for the Samaritans caught his eye, and he decided to ring the number. He found the counsellor easy to talk to, and poured out his feelings of self-loathing and hopelessness about the future. After the phone call, he felt relieved; he returned home to his parents and opened up to them. Finally, he went to see Dr Bill. After listening to Sean's story, Dr Bill realised that Sean had responded to a long period of chronic stress by becoming significantly depressed and was fortunate to have encountered the Samaritans.

Dr Bill explains how stress can lead to severe depression and offers to help Sean deal with his issues. Dr Bill recommends a holistic treatment package of exercise, proper diet, supplements and antidepressants, and finally some therapy sessions. Sean agreed to stop drinking alcohol until he was feeling better. After some time, Sean began to feel better, and Dr Bill worked with him on the issues underlying his stress and depression. Dr Bill explains the concept behind the 'ABC' approach, and together they work out the following analysis of Sean's problem:

A.   *Trigger*: Losing his job in construction.
    Inference/Danger:
- There was no hope of more employment in the foreseeable future;
- He could not get a different job, as he had no other skills;

- He had made a big mistake by leaving school early;
- There was no way out of his situation;
- He felt useless.

B. *Belief/Demands*: He was a failure.

C. *Consequences*:
Emotions: Depression.
Physical reactions: Extreme fatigue, low appetite.
Behaviour – Sean:

- worries that he will not find work again
- stops applying for jobs
- drinks too much and stops eating, and
- withdraws from family and friends.

Dr Bill then helps Sean challenge these behaviours.

CHALLENGING THE 'A' While they could challenge Sean's interpretation that he would not find a job in construction, or in another industry, because of his lack of schooling, this was a possibility.

CHALLENGING THE 'B' Dr Bill decides instead to challenge Sean's unhealthy demands and beliefs. He explains the concepts behind the 'Big MACS' but concentrates only on the rating aspect.

SELF/OTHER RATING He challenges Sean's statement that he is a failure because he can't get work in construction, and introduces him to the Raggy Doll Club.

CHALLENGING THE 'C' They decide that Sean has to accept his emotional reaction of depression, and his physical symptoms, as a normal reaction. Dr Bill challenges Sean's behavioural responses, however:

- Avoiding key decisions involving employment was only making matters worse;
- Going back into education to do his Leaving Cert, or getting additional training, would be helpful;
- Not eating, and drinking more, were not helping the situation;
- It was important for Sean to improve his diet, take supplements, and reduce his alcohol intake;
- Ruminating about his situation was not getting him anywhere;
- He could not think his way into a good situation, but he could act his way into one.

Two years later Sean is doing much better: he has completed his Leaving Cert and is going into further education in the field of electronic engineering. He is no longer stressed and depressed, is eating well, has reduced his alcohol intake, and is exercising daily. He is in a new relationship, and is doing voluntary work for a student helpline for people his own age who have got into trouble.

*

The above examples show us how toxic stress can be a great threat to our mental and physical health and how, by using the 'ABC' approach and challenging our unhealthy behaviours, we can transform our lives for the better.

Problem-solving

Before leaving this section, it would be useful to examine the concept of 'problem-solving', as this is a very useful behaviour tool when it comes to dealing with stress. Many people who suffer from chronic stress have a tendency to find themselves paralysed by indecision when it comes to choosing a course of action. This is mostly attributable to being overwhelmed by the stressor and being unable to tackle the problem in a logical manner.

Here are a few helpful hints to aid problem-solving:

- Try and break down the issues facing you into smaller, more manageable problems;
- Write out these smaller problems, decide which is the most important one, and deal with that first;
- List possible ways of dealing with this problem;
- If you cannot solve this problem, take the next one on the list, and do the same thing;
- Continue until you have decided what you can and cannot do to solve each problem;
- Focus your energy on making changes where you can, and try and ignore areas over which you have little or no control;
- Approach problems one at a time.

Here are two examples of this approach in action.

'I feel overwhelmed!'

Michael is a student who has become highly stressed because he does not think he can cover all the relevant topics for an important exam. He develops all the physical and emotional symptoms of toxic stress and engages in typical unhealthy behaviours. He visits Dr Bill, and they discuss the issue. Dr Bill takes him through the problem-solving steps listed above, and they work out the following strategy for Michael to pursue:

- First, identify the main subjects where Michael already has a good grasp of the content, and summarise the main relevant points;
- Secondly, identify areas where he needs to do more work, and tackle these areas;
- List the most common topics that arise in the exams, and prepare for these based on the notes;
- Ask lecturers what they consider to me the most important areas to focus on;
- Leave the areas he finds most difficult until last;
- Do not try to cover everything, as he will be able to remember only a certain amount;
- Focus on the most important topics, so he can revise quickly before the exam;
- In the exam itself, first put down a 'skeleton' of his answer and then flesh out the details.

The main advantage of Michael taking such an approach is that it removes his biggest difficulty: the paralysed indecision which was wasting his energy. It gives him a framework within which he should study, and reduces his stress, as he is only focusing on one thing at a time. Michael applies himself in this manner and, to his surprise, passes his exam with ease!

'I feel paralysed'

Sam is forty-five and married with two children. He has been out of work for over a year, and finds himself in a rut. His wife is bringing in some funds with her part-time job, but he has exhausted himself trying to find work in the area he was trained in – as a technician.

He has become increasingly stressed with the usual toxic-stress behaviour patterns. His wife, concerned about his mental health, sends him to see Dr Bill.

They identify that his main problem is an inability to see any way out of his present situation of unemployment, and that this is going to be it for life. Dr Bill helps him to set out the following strategy:

- He should write down all the skills he possesses, in order of importance;
- He should then list off all the passions in his life – namely interests that have always grabbed his attention and which made him feel fulfilled when he was doing them;
- Then, he should research what job opportunities there are in relation to either of these two areas;
- He should see what form of upskilling he would need in order to make his skills and passions match these job opportunities;
- If he did this, it might open up a new range of opportunities for future employment and happiness;
- He should look for any relevant professional help that was available from state organisations;

- Once he had done these things, he should return to see Dr Bill.

Two years later, Sam, who had always been very musical and loved the piano, has upskilled and set up a new school to train adults and children in the basics of piano playing. His passion has become his new vocation!

Let's now examine the last and most important step in our seven-step process: how you can put all this into action in your own life.

Step Seven

Your Life, Your 'ABC'!

Tens of thousands, or perhaps even hundreds of thousands, of people in modern Ireland are experiencing chronic stress. Many more are in danger of developing chronic stress, but may not fully appreciate the risks. You or someone close to you may be experiencing it. Let's outline the steps necessary to deal with stress. This process will target your particular problems, so you must be honest with yourself when it comes to analysing your particular situation and how it is affecting you.

Step One

You need to learn how to recognise whether or not chronic stress is actually a problem in your life. Physical symptoms are usually more immediately obvious than emotional ones. It takes real courage to face the unhealthy behaviours that accompany these symptoms, however. Here, I will outline these symptoms and behaviours again, so that you can review them and decide which relate to you. It should then become clear how chronic stress is affecting your life.

Physical symptoms:

- exhaustion
- sleep difficulties, including waking up early, grinding teeth and having nightmares
- tension headaches, often chronic
- abdominal upset, stomach cramps
- sweating, palpitations, chronic sighing and difficulty breathing
- muscle tension and pains
- bouts of viral and bacterial illnesses, including cold sores and mouth ulcers
- loss of libido
- obesity or weight loss
- restlessness, poor concentration, and difficulty finishing tasks, and
- poor short-term memory.

Psychological symptoms:

- frustration, anger and intolerance, which are characteristic of those in the high-risk group
- panic attacks and worrying
- a sense of hopelessness
- depression, negative thinking, feelings of worthlessness, and suicidal thoughts
- fixed and immutable thinking, creating conflict at home and at work

- inability to make decisions, or poor judgement, and
- addiction.

UNHEALTHY BEHAVIOURS:

- increase in smoking and alcohol consumption
- a tendency to stop exercising
- eating poorly
- misusing stimulants such as caffeine or energy drinks
- taking illegal drugs such as hash or cocaine, and
- addiction to prescription medication, such as tranquillizers, to ease anxiety.

Having identified that there is a problem, your next step involves ruling out physical and psychological illnesses which may offer an alternative explanation for your symptoms. This will require a visit to your family doctor. Such conditions include anaemia, diabetes, thyroid disease and depression.

There are two other important questions you need to ask as part of this assessment:

1. What is my family history? Is there a history of heart disease, blood pressure, diabetes, depression, addiction or anxiety?

2. Do I seem to be exhibiting any of the personality traits outlined earlier? These might predispose me a greater possibility of stress-related illnesses.

Your family history or personality may provide insight into the source of your problems and the risks you face. If a person fits into the type A personality and has a strong family history of angina or heart attacks, they are particularly at risk of experiencing serious problems if they develop chronic stress.

The next key step is to examine your lifestyle to see if any of the above unhealthy behaviours are present. Regardless of the stressor and its physical and emotional impact on an individual, these behaviours will only make the problem worse. Behaviours such as smoking, drinking, eating junk food and misusing drugs may provide short-term relief but are damaging to the person's health in the long term. If we are not prepared to change these behaviours, we remain at high risk of developing serious problems as a result of chronic stress. Other alternative therapies, such as meditation, mindfulness, yoga and pilates, can be helpful, and nutritional supplements can also reduce the negative effects of stress. Once you have identified the unhealthy behaviours relevant to you, you need to make the appropriate lifestyle changes.

Step one can be the most difficult, as it involves becoming attuned to our physical and emotional state, and being honest with ourselves regarding our lifestyle. It is worth mentioning here the significant differences between men and women in relation to how the two sexes tend to deal with this step. Men may find it more difficult to verbalise their emotions, and as a result will use a catch-all term such as 'stress', whereas women will admit to being anxious, depressed or frustrated. Men generally avoid doctors unless they are in real difficulty, and may see it as a sign of weakness in themselves to be complaining of the above symptoms. Men can also be difficult to diagnose: for example, the latest research suggests that many men with significant depression actually present with outbursts of anger.

Step Two

The next step involves writing down the stressors which we believe underly the above symptoms and behaviours. These may be related to exams, financial difficulties, relationship problems, health, sexual-identity issues, unemployment, bullying, abuse or addiction. We then need to rank the stressors in order of significance and decide which one to deal with first. You should then take the stressor in question and do an 'ABC' analysis on it, as follows:

- Take a page (see Figure 9) and divide it up into three areas, designating them as 'A', 'B' and 'C';
- Under 'A', write 'Trigger', and under that 'Inference/Danger';
- Under 'B', write 'Demands/Beliefs';
- Under 'C', write 'Consequences', and under that 'Emotions', 'Physical Symptoms' and 'Behaviours'.

We now have a simple tool to analyse exactly why a particular stressor is causing us trouble in our lives.

'I may be made redundant!'

Mary has completed step one, recognised the symptoms of chronic stress in her life, and eliminated other possibilities. She has listed five main stressors and decided that her major one is the fear that she may be made redundant.

Here is how she would approach the problem:

A.   *Trigger*: Rumours that there is due to be a meeting on the following Friday in relation to 'restructuring' the company.

Inference/Danger: Mary would ask herself the key question, 'Why is this bothering me?' and fill in the answer roughly as follows:

- If they are holding such a meeting, they may be going to lay off staff, and I might be one of those offered redundancy;
- I would then struggle, as my husband is already working part-time, and we have a significant mortgage on the house, which we would struggle to pay;
- We would get into difficulties with the bank and may end up having to fight to keep the house;
- I couldn't cope with losing the house after all the work and money we have invested in it;
- I would be letting my children down, as we would struggle to pay for many of the activities they enjoy.

B. *Belief/Demands*: Here, Mary identifies the key unhealthy beliefs and demands that are leading her to be so distressed:

- She must not be let go from her job;
- If she is let go, she will be unable to cope with the consequences;
- If she is let go, she will be a failure.

C. *Consequences*:

Emotions: Mary identifies how she feels as a consequence of her unhealthy demand above, and writes down 'anxiety' and 'low mood'.

Physical reactions: She identifies the physical symptoms she is experiencing as a result of her anxiety and low mood, and writes down 'fatigue', 'headaches', 'muscle tension' and 'stomach upset'.

Behaviour: She identifies the unhealthy behaviours which have become a response to her emotional and physical symptoms above. She notes that she:

- ruminates constantly on the fear of losing her job
- tries excessively hard to do her work perfectly
- becomes irritable with work colleagues due to exhaustion and frustration
- is sleeping poorly
- eats junk food
- smokes more cigarettes than before
- drinks more alcohol than before, and
- stops exercising.

Step Three

Now that she has outlined the problem, the next task is to examine the trigger and ask why it is bothering her. While it is sometimes obvious why an event would cause significant stress, an inaccurate interpretation of an event can also cause problems. In either case, we must evaluate the stressor in order to understand why it is a problem for us.

Let's recap on Mary's trigger, and her interpretation of it:

TRIGGER   Rumours that there is due to be a meeting the following Friday in relation to 'restructuring' the company.

Mary should then write down the evidence for her interpretation. What proof does she have that she will be laid off? While it is not beyond the realms of possibility, it is not certain to happen either. Furthermore, even if she is laid off, she has plenty of options open to her to avoid losing the family home. She also has no proof that she will end up letting her children down, or that they will be unhappy because the family is now on a tighter budget. While it is useful to challenge the 'A' in this instance, it is more helpful to challenge the demands and beliefs she places on herself.

Step Four

Here we move on to challenge our unhealthy beliefs and demands arising from our interpretation of our stressor. Let's take Mary's demands again:

B.　　Belief/Demands:
- She must not be let go from her job;
- If she is let go, she will be unable to cope with the consequences;
- If she is let go, she will be a failure.

She has made one unhealthy demand: that she must not be let go from her job. She has also stated two unhealthy beliefs: that she will not be able to cope with the consequences and that if she loses her job, she will be a failure. We can now use the 'Big MACS' to help her challenge these three unhealthy demands and beliefs.

MUST　It seems as if Mary is living in the land of 'must', which involves an absolute demand which is usually impossible to deliver. It would be healthier to use the word 'prefer', as it is more realistic. It would of course be preferable to not lose her job – but there are many things outside of Mary's control, such as the economic climate. She is demanding complete certainty that she will not lose her job, and this is not possible.

AWFUL　Mary should challenge her assumption that the worst would inevitably happen. She is visualising that her family will be out on the streets, but this scenario is unlikely to happen.

CAN'T STAND IT She believes that, if the worst did occur, she would be unable to cope. In fact, although things would be very difficult, she would almost certainly get through it for the sake of her family.

SELF/OTHER RATING Finally, she should challenge her statement that she would be a failure if she lost her job. She needs to join the Raggy Doll Club!

Step Five

Here, we move on to evaluate the emotional, physical and behavioural consequences of the unhealthy demands and beliefs we hold in response to stressors. Lets have another look at Mary's 'consequences' and see how she can challenge them.

EMOTIONS Mary identifies how she feels as a consequence of her unhealthy demand above, and writes down 'anxiety' and 'low mood'.

PHYSICAL REACTIONS She identifies the physical symptoms she is experiencing as a result of the emotions of anxiety and low mood, and writes down 'fatigue', 'headaches', 'muscle tension' and 'stomach upset'.

BEHAVIOUR Mary identifies the unhealthy behaviours which are a response to the emotions and physical symptoms outlined above, and writes them down.

It is of little help to challenge her emotional or physical responses, but it is useful to list them in order to help Mary understand how her demands and beliefs are affecting her. Mary should challenge her unhealthy behaviours as follows:

- Ruminating constantly is not helping resolve the problem;
- Being irritable with colleagues at work is not likely to increase her chances of keeping her job;
- Eating poorly, not exercising, and smoking and drinking to excess are only making her feel worse.

Mary could reduce the negative effects of toxic stress if she began to make changes along these lines. Lifestyle changes such as doing more exercise, eating properly, taking supplements, doing yoga or pilates, or going to mindfulness classes would help her greatly.

Step Six

This is where we put everything together:

- Mary has realised that she is experiencing toxic stress, after eliminating any other physical and psychological causes for the way she is feeling;
- She listed her main stressors and placed them in order of significance, and chose the one she feels is the most problematic;
- She did an 'ABC' of her problem;
- She challenged the stress trigger and analysed why it was bothering her;

- She challenged her unhealthy beliefs/demands;
- Finally, she challenged her unhealthy behaviours and resolved to change them;
- She put all these things together to create a picture of why the stressor is causing her so much difficulty and how she can deal with it most effectively.

At the end of this process, Mary has a much better idea of what is causing her problems with stress, how it is affecting her and most, importantly, how to change her thinking and behaviour in order to reduce the risks toxic stress poses to her.

To summarise our seven steps:

1. What is the main cause of toxic stress in your life?
2. What are your thoughts/emotions and behaviour in relation to the stressor? ('ABC')
3. Is your interpretation of the stressor valid
4. What unhealthy beliefs/demands are you making?
5. What are the behavioural consequences of your unhealthy beliefs?
6. Develop a working 'ABC' model;
7. Remember: *this is your life!*

Some readers will quickly grasp these steps and put them into practice in their lives, while others may seek expert help (and certainly should not be afraid of doing so!). Most of us have the capacity to handle these concepts ourselves; we just need a framework to work within. I have been amazed, from the feedback from readers of my previous books, by how quickly people in distress were able to grasp key ideas and put them into practice in their lives; dealing with stress is no different. Most of us need just three things in order to deal with stress in our lives:

- knowledge
- a simple, structured framework for dealing with the problem, and
- persistence.

To tackle stress, we need to be:

- self-observant of the symptoms and emotions arising from toxic stress
- brutally honest with ourselves in our assessment of the stressors and how we are choosing to interpret them
- brave enough to identify and challenge the key unhealthy demands and beliefs we hold, and
- strong enough to challenge the resulting unhealthy behavioural consequences.

The prize is invaluable: preventing chronic, toxic stress from wreaking physical and emotional havoc in your life. Your survival may depend upon it. The choice is yours!

Bibliography

Akil, H. (2005). 'Stressed and depressed'. *Nature Medicine*, 11, 116-118

Barry, H. P. (2009). *Flagging the Therapy: Pathways out of Depression and Anxiety*. Dublin: Liberties Press

——.(2007). *Flagging the Problem: A New Approach to Mental Health*. Dublin: Liberties Press

Brosan, L. and G. Todd (2007). *Overcoming Stress*. London: Robinson

Charney, D. S. & H. K. Manji (2004). 'Life stress, genes, and depression: Multiple pathways lead to increased risk and new opportunities for intervention'. *Science Signalling*, 225, 5

Dishman, R. K. et al (2006). 'Neurobiology of exercise'. *Obesity*, 14, 345-56

Doidge, N. (2008). *The Brain That Changes Itself*. London: Penguin Books

Ellis, A. and R. A. Harper (1975). *A Guide to Rational Living*. California: Wilshere Book Company.

Harrison, E. (2003). *The 5 Minute Meditator*. London: Piatkus

Kabat-Zinn, J. (2008). *Wherever You Go, There You Are*. London: Piatkus

Kabat-Zinn, J. (2008). *Full Catastrophe Living*. London: Piatkus

Looker, T. and O. Gregson (2003). *Teach Yourself: Managing Stress*. London: Hodder Education

Murphy, E. (2009). 'The raggy doll club'. *Forum, Journal of the Irish College of General Practitioners*

Palmer, S. and C. Cooper (2007). *How to Deal with Stress*. London: Kogan Page

Sapolsky, R. (2003). 'Taming stress'. *Scientific American*, (2003)

Williams, M. et al (2007). *The Mindful Way through Depression*. New York: the Guildford Press

Help Groups and Contact Details

Aware

Aware is a voluntary organisation established in 1985 to support those experiencing depression and their families. Aware endeavours to create a society where people with mood disorders and their families are understood and supported, and to obtain the resources to enable them to defeat depression. Weekly support group meetings at approximately fifty locations nationwide, including Northern Ireland, offer peer support and provide factual information, and enable people to gain the skills they need to help them cope with depression. Aware's 'Beat the Blues' educational programme is run in secondary schools.

Helpline: 1890 303 302
info@aware.ie | www.aware.ie | (01) 661 7211
72 Lower Leeson Street, Dublin 2

Samaritans

Samaritans was started in 1953 in London by a young vicar called Chad Varah; the first branch in the Republic of Ireland opened in Dublin in 1970. Samaritans provides a twenty-four-hour-a-day confidential service offering emotional support for people who are experiencing feelings of distress or despair, including those which may lead to suicide.

Helpline: 1850 60 90 90
jo@samaritans.org | www.samaritans.org
Texts: 0872 60 90 90

Grow

Established in Ireland in 1969, GROW is Ireland's largest mutual-help organisation in the area of mental health. It is anonymous, nondenominational, confidential and free. No referrals are necessary. Grow aims to achieve self-activation through mutual help. Its members are enabled, over time, to craft a step-by-step recovery or personal-growth plan, and to develop leadership skills that will help others.

Helpline: 1890 474 474
grownational@grow.ie | www.grow.ie | 056 61624
Barrack Street, Kilkenny

Irish Suicidology Association

The Irish Association of Suicidology aims to facilitate communication between clinicians, volunteers, survivors and researchers in all matters relating to suicide and suicidal behaviour; to promote awareness of the problems of suicide and suicidal behaviour in the general public by holding conferences and workshops and through the communication of relevant materials through the media; to ensure that the public is better informed about suicide prevention; to support and encourage relevant research; and to encourage and support the formation of groups to help those bereaved by suicide.

094 925 0858 | office@ias.ie | www.ias.ie
16 New Antrim Street, Castlebar, County Mayo

Console

Console is a registered charity supporting and helping people bereaved through suicide. They respect each individual's unique journey through the grieving process following their tragic loss. Console promotes positive mental health within the community in an effort to reduce the high number of attempted suicides and deaths through suicide.

Helpline: 1800 201 890
info@console.ie | www.console.ie | 01 857 4300
Console Dublin: All Hallows College,
Gracepark Rd, Drumcondra, Dublin 9

Rainbows Ireland

Rainbows was founded in America by Suzy Yehl Marta to help children and adults who have been bereaved through parental death, separation or divorce to work through the grieving process which follows any significant loss. The charity provides a safe setting in which children can talk through their feelings with other children who are experiencing similar situations.

01 473 4175
Loreto Centre, Crumlin Road, Dublin 12

ChildLine

ChildLine, a service run by the ISPCC, seeks to empower and support children using the medium of telecommunications and information technology. The service is designed for all children and young people up to the age of eighteen in Ireland.

Helpline: 1890 66 66 66

Cuan Mhuire

Cuan Mhuire is a charitable organisation founded by Sister Consilio Fitzgerald in 1965. It provides a comprehensive structured, abstinence-based residential programme dealing with alcohol, gambling and drug addiction in the north and south of Ireland, with centres in Athy, Athenry, Newry, Limerick and Cork.

063 00555 | cuanmhuire@gmail.com

Gamblers Anonymous Ireland and Gam-Anon

Holds self-help meetings for gamblers and those close to them.

Dublin 01 872 1133
Cork 087 349 4450
Galway 087 349 4450
info@gamblersanonymous.ie

Al-Anon / Alateen

Self-help meetings for spouses and teenagers (aged twelve to seventeen) affected by those addicted to alcohol.

01 873 2699 | info@al-anon-ireland.org
5 Capel Street, Dublin 1

028 9068 2368
Peace House, 224 Lisburn Road, Belfast

Narcotics Anonymous

Self-help groups for those addicted to drugs.

01 672 8000 | na@ireland.org
4–5 Eustace Street, Dublin 2

The Irish Council for Psychotherapy

Produces a directory of psychotherapists working in Ireland.

01 272 2105 | info@icpty.ie
73 Quinns Road, Shankhill, County Dublin

Schizophrenia Ireland

Schizophrenia Ireland is the national organisation dedicated to upholding the rights and addressing the needs of all those affected by enduring mental illness, including schizophrenia, schizo-affective disorder and bipolar disorder, through the promotion and provision of high-quality services, and by working to ensure the continual enhancement of the quality of life of the people it serves.

01 860 1620 | info@sirl.ie
38 Blessington Street, Dublin 7

The Irish Association of Cognitive Behavioural Therapy

This organisation was founded in 2003 by Enda Murphy and Brian Kelly. Its primary aim is the provision of low-intensity CBT/CBM training and support to health professionals and organisations for use in their clinical practice.

cbtireland@eircom.net

No Panic

No Panic is a charity which aims to faclitate the relief and rehabilitation of people suffering from panic attacks, phobias, obsessive compulsive disorders and other related anxiety disorders, including tranquillizer withdrawal, and to provide support to sufferers and their families and carers. Founded by Colin M. Hammond in the UK, this group has extended its activities to Ireland, where it is organised by therapist Caroline McGuigan.

Helpline Ireland: 01 272 1897
UK head office: TEL: +44 (0) 1952 590005
FAX: +44 (0) 1952 270962
Helpline (UK Free-Phone): 0808 808 0545
Non-UK: 0044 1 952 590545
Ireland office: 01 272 1872

Headstrong

Headstrong is a new initiative spearheaded by psychologist Dr Tony Bates, working with communities in Ireland to ensure that young people aged twelve to twenty-five are better supported to achieve mental health and well-being. Headstrong was set up in response to an identified need to address the issue of youth mental health in Ireland. It is an independent, non-profit NGO. It acts as an expert partner to the Health Services Executive and other people and services concerned with providing mental health and well-being support to young people in Ireland. Headstrong views mental health as existing along a continuum spanning general well-being to distress to mental health disorders that require specialised care. Headstrong's Jigsaw Programme aims to change the way communities in Ireland think about mental health and support young people in the process.

www.headstrong.ie | info@headstrong.ie | 01 6607343
36 Waterloo Road, Ballsbridge, Dublin 4

Memoirs of a Medical Maverick
by Risteárd Mulcahy

'A moving memoir' – *Sunday Independent*

Risteárd Mulcahy – internationally renowned cardiologist and health campaigner, researcher, historian, exercise enthusiast and environmentalist – was born into a tight-knit south Dublin community at a time of innocence and conformity. This autobiography is a unique and often surprising insight into the rich, varied and extraordinary life of one of the most prominent, respected and outspoken medical men in Ireland.

Medical Maverick charts the personal and professional life of a true Irish progressive – from his modest childhood in Rathmines (complete with cows, chickens and armed guards outside the family home) to his university days in Dublin and post-war London, his early career delivering babies in some of Dublin's worst slums, his later health-promotion activities and discusses with candid authority some of the most pressing health issues our time. Risteárd Mulcahy emerges as someone who – whether in success or failure – has always lived an admirably active and inquisitive life.

Available at bookshops nationwide and online at www.LibertiesPress.com

€17.99 | ISBN: 978-1-907593-02-4